# DANCE PARTNERING BASICS

## Practical Skills and Inclusive Pedagogy

**BRANDON WHITED, MFA**
UNIVERSITY OF CALIFORNIA, SANTA BARBARA

WITH **JOSHUA MANCULICH, MFA**

 HUMAN KINETICS

**Library of Congress Cataloging-in-Publication Data**

Library of Congress Cataloging-in-Publication Data
Names: Whited, Brandon, 1985- author. | Manculich, Joshua, 1987- author.
Title: Dance partnering basics : practical skills and inclusive pedagogy /
Brandon Whited, MFA, University of California, Santa Barbara, with
Joshua Manculich, MFA.
Description: Champaign, IL : Human Kinetics, [2025] | Includes
bibliographical references and index.
Identifiers: LCCN 2023021740 (print) | LCCN 2023021741 (ebook) | ISBN
9781492598060 (paperback : alk. paper) | ISBN 9781492598077 (epub) |
ISBN 9781492598084 (pdf)
Subjects: LCSH: Dance--Social aspects. | Exercise.
Classification: LCC GV1588.6 .W535 2025  (print) | LCC GV1588.6 (ebook) |
DDC 792.8--dc23/eng/20230817
LC record available at https://lccn.loc.gov/2023021740
LC ebook record available at https://lccn.loc.gov/2023021741

ISBN: 978-1-4925-9806-0 (print)

**Acquisitions Editor:** Bethany J. Bentley
**Developmental Editor:** Melissa Feld
**Managing Editor:** Melissa J. Zavala
**Copyeditor:** Christina West
**Proofreader:** A.E. Williams
**Indexer:** Andrea J. Hepner
**Permissions Manager:** Laurel Mitchell
**Senior Graphic Designer:** Nancy Rasmus
**Cover Designer:** Keri Evans
**Cover Design Specialist:** Susan Rothermel Allen
**Photograph (cover and title page):** © Fritz Olenberger
**Photographs (interior):** © Human Kinetics, unless otherwise noted
**Photo Asset Manager:** Laura Fitch
**Photo Production Specialist:** Amy M. Rose
**Photo Production Manager:** Jason Allen
**Senior Art Manager:** Kelly Hendren
**Illustrations:** © Human Kinetics, unless otherwise noted
**Printer:** Sheridan Books
Printed in the United States of America      10  9  8  7  6  5  4  3  2  1

The paper in this book is certified under a sustainable forestry program.

| **Human Kinetics** | *United States and International* | *Canada* |
|---|---|---|
| 1607 N. Market Street | Website: **US.HumanKinetics.com** | Website: **Canada.HumanKinetics.com** |
| Champaign, IL 61820 | Email: info@hkusa.com | Email: info@hkcanada.com |
| USA | Phone: 1-800-747-4457 | |

E8065

THIS BOOK IS DEDICATED to all those who feel, or have ever felt, alone and isolated in this world. I hope you find your way back to yourself and find meaningful ways to connect with others.

# CONTENTS

# PREFACE

Partnering is a vital, foundational aspect of dance that is present in social and ballroom dance practice and performance, commercial dance, and most genres of concert dance. If dance serves as a reflection of the human condition, dance partnering is key to demonstrating relationships, human connection, and interaction. With such a broad presence in many facets of the field, why is the practice of dance partnering significantly underrepresented in dance education?

This question served as a catalyst for the creation of this book, *Dance Partnering Basics: Practical Skills and Inclusive Pedagogy*, as a resource for dance educators and students to discover the possibilities and positive impact of dedicated dance partnering practice. Teachers in K-12, higher education, and private studio sectors and students of dance and dance education at the undergraduate and graduate levels will all find helpful information about how to begin or further dance partnering offerings within their curriculum or personal practice. By drawing from varied and divergent trainings in partnering forms, this book (1) offers practical skill-based techniques and cross-training for injury prevention, (2) tactics for incorporating partnered work into improvisation and creative or choreographic courses, (3) considers the implications of touch for students of varied ages and experience levels, and (4) discusses the importance and benefits of inclusive pedagogy.

This book originated from a dance partnering pedagogy workshop presented at the 2018 National Dance Education Organization National Conference, recognizing the dearth of practical pedagogical information specifically tailored to the study and practice of dance partnering (Manculich and Whited 2018). The seed idea for this foundational workshop stemmed from anecdotal realization that many programs around the country have not prioritized dance partnering as a vital aspect of core curricular requirements and training regimens. From the private studio sector to higher education, partnering is often only addressed within the context of repertory or the creation of new work. Departments and programs often rely on the interest and expertise of guest teaching artists or guest choreographers to cover these fundamentals when partnering is an integral part of their choreographic voice or aesthetic. Even within the professional field of concert dance—when speaking with numerous artistic directors, freelance choreographers, and rehearsal directors—it is common to encounter highly trained, exceptional dancer-artists who have little or no training in dance partnering. At worst, this significant gap in their training can lead to job loss or limit the type of work in which they might be cast; at best, this gap may require the choreographer or peer company members to first teach fundamental mechanics of partnering before approaching repertory or the creation of new work. In a time of pick-up performances and project-based dance companies, limited time and financial resources do not often allow for that additional training to occur.

For these practical reasons, along with a list of relatable skills learned through the practice of dance partnering, a concerted effort can (and I argue, *should*) be made to incorporate dance partnering training into the fabric of college curricula, dance studio practices, and more. This applies even to students not seeking a path in the professional concert dance field. *Dance Partnering Basics* provides a springboard of skills and perspectives that might inspire dance educators in all sectors to incorporate peer-to-peer and group-based dance partnering technique, exploration, and experiences into their varied training practices. It takes a broad, multimodal approach to foundational dance partnering pedagogy that can apply across genres.

This book also sheds light on the deep value and broad-reaching benefits of teaching dance partnering without a restrictive and limiting approach to gender. To date, the primary dance partnering print and video resources focus almost entirely on the singular practice of ballet partnering and its famed pas de deux—with formal, traditional approaches to partnering rooted heavily in a binaried, gendered view and application of the male and female divide. This rigidly gender-normative stance, which privileges partnering between a man and a woman and limits discussion of each gendered role in partnering to what they should know and be trained for, restricts students from reaching their full potential and understanding in both supportive and supported roles in partnering.

*Dance Partnering Basics* offers an inclusive view of dance partnering that discusses the dichotomies of supported partner and supportive partner, leader and follower, and giver and receiver rather than the narrow male and female gender binary. This approach allows dance educators serving a range of student populations to successfully engage their students and instill a strong foundation for any dance partnering form. Along with providing practical ways to foster an inclusive partnering classroom, this book addresses changes in identity and expression as well as the interpersonal politics and negotiation of consent and touch.

*Dance Partnering Basics* is organized around the foundational elements of dance—time, weight, energy and flow, and space—as a means of creatively grouping the varied aspects one might consider when honing or developing partnering offerings. Included throughout the text are individual exercise breakdowns to offer practical approaches to teaching fundamentals and mechanics. Although the exercises are broadly linked to each chapter's focus, they are also organized in an overarching progression, with one building on the other as skills are learned and explored. These exercises are presented in three parts (I, II, and III) in the Practical Skills and Frameworks for Teaching Dance Partnering series in chapters 2 through 4, respectively. *Practical skills* refer to the techniques, mechanics, and individual partnered skills shared within these sections, and *frameworks* refer to the guided improvisations, creative explorations, and broader teaching methods one might use to effectively lead a partnering class. Within the individual exercises, variations and more advanced versions are offered. Readers should feel empowered and invited to rename, reframe, redesign, expand, and adapt any or all parts of the exercises offered. A unique aspect of contemporary dance is the naming and renaming of individual movements, phrases, or even sections of dances when not rooted in a codified system such as ballet or foundational modern techniques. Teachers can tailor the naming and framing of exercises or iterations of explorations relative to their dance backgrounds and cultural orientations.

## Chapter Overview

A brief overview of each chapter follows.

**Chapter 1, Introduction to Dance Partnering,** provides a concise history and explanation of dance partnering forms and considers broad implications for the practice as a vital and powerful component of dance education and training. This chapter frames the characteristics of different genres to create a foundational understanding of varied methods, approaches, and frameworks in partnering. Chapter 1 also provides a practical overview of the text and its ancillary resources to assist teachers in the navigation of its reading and application within the studio.

**Chapter 2, Time: Getting Started,** serves the early stages of imagining and implementing dance partnering training into programs, curricula, and personal practices. Broad ideas about class planning and course development, sample syllabi and foundational vocabulary, and concepts and teaching techniques offer a springboard into the more specific content in later chapters. Chapter 2 includes part I of the Practical Skills and Frameworks for Teaching Dance Partnering series, which introduces fundamental exercises of connection, weight sensing, and weight-bearing with low risk and low momentum.

**Chapter 3, Weight: Digging Deeper,** considers the body as an instrument, with discussions of safe techniques and foundational biomechanics; frameworks for cross-training and preparatory strengthening for partnering students; promotion of self-care, proper nutrition, and dancer wellness; and, when appropriate, techniques for partnered somatic body work, mutual care, and maintenance. Chapter 3 presents part II of the Practical Skills and Frameworks for Teaching Dance Partnering series, which furthers the foundational skills from part I with more advanced and complex principles and includes more traditional approaches to dance partnering.

**Chapter 4, Energy and Flow: Activating Creativity,** explores partnering within the contexts of creative practices. Where partnering training is lacking, often the creative work and improvisational approaches of students include little-to-no physical, partnered elements. This chapter offers tactics, exercises, and choreographic prompts to help students to unlock their creativity and confidence in using partnering and weight-bearing elements in their choreography or improvisational practices. Further examples are offered to foster and develop awareness and skills for group partnering. Once students have a practical and technical tool kit and a broader understanding of what is possible, their capacity to dream, create, and actualize partnering in their work will blossom. Chapter 4 includes part III of the Practical Skills and Frameworks for Teaching Dance Partnering series, which presents the most layered and advanced partnering principles offered in the exercises in this book.

**Chapter 5, Space: Fostering Community and Inclusive Pedagogy,** gets to the heart of dance partnering and dance education philosophies more broadly by considering questions like these: What sort of class culture and space do teachers want to foster and provide for their students? What toxic practices in their training do teachers wish to avoid or reframe to create a better environment for their students and peers? How can teachers open the door for all students to feel safe, supported, and welcome? Suggestions are provided for establishing a safe space, fostering a supportive environment, and creating a community within the classroom and beyond. This chapter furthers these considerations by suggesting inclusive pedagogical practices, encouraging awareness of differences, and modeling the use of gender-neutral language and practices within the classroom. Chapter 5 also considers the dynamics of touch and consent, and it cultivates inclusion through embracing differences and respecting diverse identities.

## Practical Skills and Frameworks for Teaching Dance Partnering

Chapters 2 through 4 include the three parts dedicated to Practical Skills and Frameworks for Teaching Dance Partnering. These parts are separated into individual and grouped exercises that provide specific information about how to introduce, explore, implement, and connect the techniques and mechanics of a range of skills within dance partnering.

Each exercise in chapters 2 through 4 is designed to build on the skills of the exercises that precede it. For many, the exercises and the amount of variations for exploring them become more complex as they progress. The first few exercises in chapter 2 have less instruction on preparation and foundational exercises, as they serve that function for more complex work later on.

The exercises are organized as follows:

- *Background.* Each exercise is framed by a background section that describes the origins or conceptual basis for a given exercise. These sections also include credits and specific lineages of ideas when possible, and all are framed within the perspective of my own experience as the principles were introduced to me over the course of my training and professional career.

- *Purpose.* The purpose sections frame the goals and expected outcomes intended for the practice of a particular exercise. Although these may vary in practice for educators in different teaching venues, the learning potential remains largely the same.

As the exercises progress and become more complex in their own right, preparatory warm-ups, exercises, and explorations are offered to prepare students for the full expression of the skill being learned.

- *Foundational Exercises.* These exercises are suggested warm-ups, tune-ups, or organized ways to explain a technique to students before they engage a partner.

- *Guided Improvisations.* These suggested prompts help educators to lead students through individual, partnered, or group explorations of a movement principle or concept. The use of an improvisational framework allows students to work within their comfort zone as they become familiar with the technique. For many students, having room to find their own way into a concept helps them become more comfortable and confident earlier in the practice.

- *Workshopping.* These sections outline ideas for using a more directed, organized approach to exploring a skill or movement technique. By isolating a specific movement or narrowing the field of possibilities, the instructor can home in on the approach that students need to take when practicing the exercise.

- *In Practice.* These sections outline the core practice of a particular skill or exercise. In this central part of the exercise, key concepts and considerations are explained, and variations are offered to deepen and further the practice of a particular exercise.

- *Modifications and Problem-Solving.* Information is offered for instructors who need to simplify the material for a truly beginning population of students. Common pitfalls and challenges are offered as a means to preemptively anticipate them and watch for students who are having difficulty with an exercise.

- *Expanding and Advanced Skills.* These sections offer suggestions on how to make an exercise more challenging for students who have advanced skills or are quickly progressing. Increased risk, momentum, and complexity allow for a more nuanced and accelerated practice of a given exercise. In some classes, the instructor may need to accommodate modifications for some students while offering more challenging directions to others.

It seems important to state plainly that this book in no way represents the entirety of dance partnering knowledge, nor does it directly address the needs of all student populations and groups. The information and approaches represented herein are drawn from more than 30 years and varied personal experience in dance partnering forms primarily situated in training lineages of western concert dance. The practical aspects of the book are offered as a foundation of skills and mechanics that any educator can then infuse with their own aesthetics, style, and cultural perspective, or to tailor instruction to the needs of a specific population of students.

It should also be noted that due to the practice-based nature of dance training, dancers are continually influenced and inspired by the many teachers, choreographers, collaborators, and peers with whom they interact. These traces and influences are often clear in one's technical and artistic approach, but are also subconscious and unnameable. The content in this resource is offered as a confluence of ideas and practices learned, explored, developed, refined, and revisited over many years of performing, creating, and teaching. To the degree possible, context and credit to original sources or influences is plainly stated in the text, but there are inevitably many more that color and temper the content in the book.

Although there are numerous approaches to teaching dance partnering, selecting material, and implementing its inclusion in dance curricula within varied settings, this book aims to help readers zoom out and consider the broad potential of a dedicated dance partnering practice, and zoom in to consider the building blocks and individual techniques that might constitute a rounded study of partnering. *Dance Partnering Basics* offers just one of the many perspectives and approaches possible within dance partnering training and, hopefully, may inspire even more scholar-educators to share their experiences and points of view in this vastly underrepresented but central aspect of dance training.

# HK*PROPEL* ACCESS AND VIDEO CONTENTS

*Dance Partnering Basics* includes access to HK*Propel*, which includes video demonstrating the dance partnering exercises, workouts, and strengthening and breathing exercises. You'll find references to the video in chapters 2, 3, and 4 marked with this play button icon ▶. In addition to the video, HK*Propel* includes reflection question for the instructor, discussion questions for the student, class plans, and suggested writing prompts and assignments.

To access HK*Propel*, see the card at the front of the print book for your unique HK*Propel* access code. For ebook users, reference the HK*Propel* access code instructions on the page immediately following the book cover.

## Chapter 2

Yoga Ball as Partner

Partnered Surfing Exercise

Body Mapping With Passive Mobilization

Active and Passive

Weight Sharing

Counterbalance

Shelves and Ledges

## Chapter 3

Isometric Positions With Mobility Challenges

  High plank windshield wipers

  High plank shin-ups

  Lawn mowers from side plank

  Scapula push-ups

  Bear crawl

Lower Body–Focused Challenges

  One-legged hops

  Two-legged hops

  Burpees

  Squat jumps

  Mountain climbers

  Double lunges

  Parallel skaters or glissades

Lower Body Workout

360-Degree Core Workout

Upper Body Workout

Zoned Tactile Breathing

Partnered Zoned Tactile Breathing

Exploring Draping

Airplane Demonstration

Redirection and Leverage

U-Turn Redirection Lift

Backward Flight Lift

Over, Under, and Through

Rocking Chair Improvisation

Falling and Rocking

Assisted Inversions

# Chapter 4

# ACKNOWLEDGMENTS

First, thank you to **Josh Manculich** for your herculean contribution to the genesis, evolution, and initial manuscript development of this book. You know how much I appreciate you as a colleague and friend. I couldn't have done it without you. Thank you for all the trips out West to have dedicated writing retreats and for your ongoing encouragement and support related to this project, and all of my personal and professional endeavors.

Dancers owe a great deal of gratitude to the teachers, coaches, directors, and choreographers who influence us through the years. Thank you to **all my teachers and mentors** along the way. You lifted me up, challenged me, and selflessly shared your wisdom and experience in the service of my growth and that of all of your students.

Thank you, in particular, to my dedicated partnering teachers. Your patience, guidance, and passion fostered in me a deep love of dance and partnering specifically. **Michelle Killman** marks the beginning of my journey with dance. I am forever grateful for my great fortune in walking into that dance studio and having the privilege to learn from you. You brought a rigor and drive into the studio and shared your worldly experience of life and dance with all of us. You were always encouraging and inspiring me, yet pushing me to hold myself to the highest standard for growth and improvement.

Thank you to **Sean Sullivan**, my teacher and mentor in undergraduate studies at the University of North Carolina School of the Arts (UNCSA) who helped me refine my early experience with dance partnering and elevating that technique and perspective to meet the professional world. You were also my first male dance teacher, which had a profound influence on the way I viewed myself and my place in the dance field. You introduced me to contact improvisation, modern and contemporary partnering, and so much more. By getting to work with you on multiple pieces, I was able to gain even more insight into your artistry, your skillful technique, and the passion you have for dance.

To **Teri and Oliver Steele**—who I met and worked with on two separate occasions while doing my undergraduate studies at UNCSA and for whom I later danced for seven years as a freelancer in their company, Steeledance—thank you for everything. Rooted in my time working with you both during such formative years, I learned so much about partnering composition and movement development from you. Beyond that, the open, inclusive environment you fostered in your classes and company culture solidified a deep pride in my own uniqueness and difference, which you celebrated at every turn. Thanks also to my partners in the company. Over the years performing with you, I learned so much about nonverbal connection, reciprocal leadership within a partnership, and seamless adaptability.

I owe a huge debt of gratitude to **Shen Wei**, whose vision, rigor, and creativity are boundless sources of inspiration to me. You unlocked a whole new perspective on the nuance, delicacy, and duration that partnering can express, and you introduced me to a way of dancing that felt (and continues to feel) like home in my body. Thank you to my many peers and partners from Shen Wei Dance Arts. I learned so much from each of you, both directly and within the privilege of watching you work at such a high level of professionalism and artistry.

Thank you, thank you to the inimitable **Bebe Miller**, who broke open my notions of what partnering is and can be. You always got to the root and essence of the dynamics of human connection and relationality. Your esoteric yet razor-sharp questions always challenge one to think more creatively and to continually interrogate what is felt and what is "known."

Thanks also to all of the faculty educators and mentors I had the privilege of working with during my graduate studies at **The Ohio State University** (OSU). You helped me reconnect with my passion and curiosity in dance, allowed me to revisit the study of dance from an intellectual place, and helped me find my interest and potential as an educator and creative artist in my own right.

Many thanks to my dear friends from my OSU graduate cohort and to the cohorts that came before and after. You all touched my life in so many ways and fueled my entry into academia.

An epic thank you to my publishing and editorial team from Human Kinetics. I have so appreciated your guidance, kindness, grace, patience, understanding, and encouragement along the way. Were it not for your interest and encouragement to turn that initial partnering workshop into this book, it might never have happened.

Finally, thank you to my family and close friends. You have always been there. In recitals, music concerts and plays early on, in the audience at performances and talkbacks during my professional years, and even humoring me during my mini lectures (rants) at the dinner table on holiday visits. Your support and encouragement never falters.

*With love and gratitude, I thank you!*

UCSB students performing in *Ragtime Suite*.
Choreography by Brandon Whited.

# 1

# INTRODUCTION TO DANCE PARTNERING

## OVERVIEW

This chapter provides a concise history of dance partnering, introduces the forms described in this book, and outlines the practical and creative potential of partnering practice in dance education and training. By framing the development of dance partnering forms and the characteristics of different styles, this chapter provides a foundational understanding of multiple methods, approaches, and frameworks in partnering. The roots of dance partnering can be traced to many global dance practices from different eras. This book is limited to lineages that led directly to partnering practices in contact improvisation, ballet, modern dance, and contemporary dance. Although a comprehensive historiography of dance partnering's evolution is sorely needed in the dance studies canon, this chapter merely touches on dance partnering's historical roots to provide context for the skills and potential of the forms described here. This chapter also provides a practical overview of the book, along with its components and ancillary resources, and suggestions for how to navigate, adapt, and use these offerings in practice.

### VOCABULARY

ballroom dance

classicism

contact improvisation

court dance

modernism

neoclassicism

postmodernism

social dance

Broadly speaking, dance partnering directly reflects the human need to know, understand, love, relate to, connect with, and bond with other people. Consider how this need manifests in daily life: How do people relate to their family members? How do they connect, communicate, and share intimate moments with a romantic partner or close friends? How do people interact with colleagues and clients or with strangers? At its roots, partnering is the aspect of dance that reflects these shared human experiences of connection to another individual or multiple individuals within a group.

## Brief History of Dance Partnering Forms and Lineage

This chapter begins a dedicated study of dance partnering and its pedagogical potential, so it is important to consider its origins and development. The evolution of dance as a vital cultural practice and creative form of expression spans several millennia and cultural and historical periods, which have been studied widely and written about extensively. Clear tracings of the development of dance partnering with its own history, traditions, and evolution over time are harder to locate in the dance history canon. The purpose here is not to delve into the historical lineage of dance partnering. Rather, this book examines the development of partnering as it evolved within important sociocultural histories—both within and outside of performing arts contexts. Dance partnering traces back to historical and indigenous dance forms, which were later formed inside the European courts and incorporated national, culturally specific dance traditions. Partnered dancing was later codified and developed within ballroom dance and classical ballet training. In the mid-20th century, partnered dancing experienced significant shifts with the development of the modern, postmodern, and contemporary dance movements.

To examine the roots of dance partnering practice, it is necessary to first identify what it is to dance together. Consider these questions: Must there be direct contact? Does direct interaction via two dancers' attention and energy constitute partnered interaction? Can group rituals and celebratory dance forms be considered partnered forms? These community-based forms of partnered dance interaction are discussed in chapter 5, which addresses creating and fostering community. For the broad historical reflection presented here, it is important to look to the dynamics of restriction and repression in time periods in which touch and direct contact between and among the sexes was regulated in religious, social, and moral codes (Horst 1953). In those spaces, dance partnering was limited in its ability to emerge and evolve because of restricted interaction between dancers in observance of social morals and values. Many culturally specific, historical dance practices are organized into separate, binary-gendered movement vocabularies that contrast with community-building dances performed by large groups. Common examples are found in West African dance, European national dance forms, East and South Asian dances, and the Pacific Islands. Many of these ritual, ceremonial, and historical social dances are organized with movement material and common dances designed solely for men or women to perform, and they are practiced and performed in groups or as solos by masters of the forms. In the time periods from which such traditional forms emerged, binary-gendered dances were often framed as a reflection of daily life and social practices, with roles and responsibilities assigned separately to men and women. To be sure, anomalous examples can be identified when history is considered in exhaustive detail. But broadly speaking, gendered separations can be found within the cultural dances of many global communities, time periods, and sociocultural frames (Nevile 2007).

# European Court Dance: Side-by-Side Partnered Interactions

The roots of the more formal aspects of dance partnering referenced in this book are most easily traced to the 17th- and 18th-century European court dances. Court dance developed most significantly during the Renaissance, and it often evolved from formalized, aristocratically neutralized versions of regional dances emerging from communities in rural Europe. Where the origination of the dances was often exemplified by informal and secular expressions of their culture, the dancing masters of the European courts appropriated and neutralized these dances to be appropriate for performance in the aristocratic, often repressive, European courts of the time.

Most of these social dances, reframed in monarchical social spaces as court dances, maintained socially and religiously appropriate interactions between the sexes with a side-by-side orientation that kept them celibately safe at arm's length. Much like their original forms developed in regionally and nationally specific cultures, many of these large, group-based, partnered dances were performed for courtly, ceremonial purposes. Some dances were sanitized and simplified to be considered acceptable and appropriate within the formality of the European courts. The gavotte, for example, originated in Gap, "a district in the Upper Alps in the ancient province of Dauphine, in south-eastern France," and kisses between dancers were replaced with the offering of bouquets when introduced as a dance within the French court (Horst 1953).

The pavane and minuet were large group processional dances (Horst 1953). Because they were slow in tempo and characterized by a simple and narrow range of steps suitable for performance by individuals of all ages with varied experience, these dances allowed

*Nvove inventioni di balli*, Italian court dance.
Retrieved from the Library of Congress, www.loc.gov/item/12018603/.

for broad inclusion and involvement among members of the court. With more nuance, skill, and robust energy required, other dances such as the galliard, courante, gigue, and bourrée became the subject of dedicated and formal practice of the growing technique of court dancing. One court dance that can be most easily pointed to as a precursor to the aerial lifting and partnering in classical ballet is the volté, a form of the galliard characterized by exuberant lifts and spins of the women, who were supported by the strength and vigor of the men at court. The volté was a favorite of Queen Elizabeth I (1533-1603) and one of her primary forms of exercise, although the dance was ill-favored by the religious and moral watchdogs of the time (Horst 1953). Dances that went beyond the formality of hand-to-hand contact were often disregarded as secular and scandalous.

As explained in *Social Dance: A Brief History*, A.H. Franks identifies the emergence of the waltz as a significant turning point in the development of court dance and ballroom dance forms. Most notable was the use of a closed-hold frame between dancers, in which the male dancer (leading) and female dancer (following) connected to one another in a closed loop between arms and bodies, which was scandalous at the time. Leaving the chaste formality of a side-by-side frame connected only by the hands of greatly extended arms, the waltz closed off the dancers from outside spectators and brought about new intimacy and heightened sexuality in public dancing. While the waltz is unlikely to be considered sexy and scandalous today, it was exactly that in the early 19th-century culture of the formal, aristocratic courts. Franks explains that "the dance was not a product of the century, and appears to have been born in the suburbs of Vienna and in the Alpine districts of Austria" (Franks 1963, 127). "The climate was not yet suitable" in the middle of the 17th century when it emerged initially, "and not until the Industrial Revolution was well underway did the time become ripe for the true flowering of the dance" (Franks 1963, 127). In a comprehensive expression of the significance of the waltz, Franks points to the frame or closed-hold position as a key shift in social dance:

> Various writers have made the point that with the waltz there was also introduced into the social dance the closed hold which has exerted such a powerful influence upon most social forms of dance ever since. It would perhaps have been more correct to refer to this feature as a "reintroduction" for as far back as the sixteenth century we have seen that in at least one dance, La Volta, a similar kind of hold was in favor. At the outset this so-called closed hold in the Waltz was of a sufficiently circumspect nature to allow ample "daylight" between the couples, and it was not for about a hundred years that dancers became so daring as to allow their bodies actually to come into close contact with each other as they rotated giddily round the floor. (Franks 1963, 130)

As the dances of European courts became more popular, the role of the dancing master emerged in the form of experienced dancers with a propensity for teaching. The masters eventually arranged dances to be performed by the court, coached prominent individuals, and introduced new regional dances made appropriate for performance in front of the monarchs. In his formative manual, *The Dancing Master*, originally printed in 1725, Pierre Rameau (1674-1748) clearly outlined the accepted customs, positions, rhythms, steps, and pathways of the formal dances of the French court. As one of several master teachers at the time, Rameau was particularly well positioned to speak to the shift in formal dance technique from performative court dancing toward the dramatic narratives of ballet within the multifaceted artform of opera that would develop into the storytelling ballet form known today. Like many dancing masters (often French within various European courts), Rameau instructed and coached dancers within the courts of Louis XIV of France (1638-1715) and was the personal dancing master to Elizabeth Farnese who married Philip V of Spain in 1714 (Beaumont 2003).

As Jennifer Nevile explains in *The Cambridge Companion to Ballet*, dancing masters emerged because "a high level of skill was needed in order to perform gracefully in public without error." She further notes that "a dancer had to be able to learn the correct carriage of the body, to master the steps and their many variants and to [memorize] the choreographies" (Nevile 2007, 12). As dancing became more popular in the court and was favored by many monarchs, the social and political necessity of excellence in the social grace was paramount for the aristocracy of the time. To learn the basic skills, continue to refine and progress their technique and performance ability, and keep up with current trends, steps, dances, and styles, many turned to the private tutelage of the dancing masters.

Throughout the 17th and 18th centuries, the progression of court dance styles, techniques, and practices evolved significantly, often drawing from regional dances developed via culturally specific practices of rural and suburban communities in Europe. The shift in court dance toward what is now referred to as the foundations of classical ballet is most often attributed to King Louis XIV (1638-1715), also known as Louis the Great or the Sun King. He was a fervent supporter of the development of the arts during his reign and had a particular love for, and prowess in, dancing (Beaumont 2003). It was not until the arrival of Italian-born composer Jean-Baptiste Lully (1632-1687) and the introduction of opera that formal dance performance, framed by narrative storylines and executed for an audience, became the precursor to what is now considered classical ballet. As Rameau explains in *The Dancing Master*, "dancing did not appear in its full glory until the birth of Opera" (Beaumont 2003, xii).

French King Louis XIV (1638-1715), the Sun King, in the role of Apollo.
Bibliotheque nationale de France.

With the imposition of the narrative, dramatic storytelling of opera, dance developed as well. This led to the inclusion of more direct partnering within the opera ballets to tell romantic, heroic, mythic, and dramatic stories through the roles of princes, queens, gods, and goddesses and the necessary depictions of their relationships, development, and (often) tragic ends. The shift from the formal, technical application of court dance for individuals to demonstrate status, prowess, and social relevance toward opera with its stories, protagonists, and relational dynamics was fertile ground for further development in the classical ballet tradition.

## Classical and Neoclassical Ballet

As ballet evolved, the technical demands on dancers increased as notable dancers became well known for unique performative attributes or skill execution. Individualistic styles and technical approaches from influential choreographers also led to the development of technical skill broadly, but similarly affected dance partnering approaches within classical ballet. Marius Petipa (1818-1910) and Lev Ivanov (1834-1901) are some of the most famous choreographers of the time and inspired the next generation. With balletic styles emerging and developing differently within different European nations, the aesthetic, technique, story, and storytelling all had bearing on what was required of dancers within partnering contexts.

Within the early traditions of ballet classicism that emerged from the French and Italian courts and later developed further in England, Imperial Russia, and elsewhere, dance partnering found its expression through the formal device of the pas de deux. With earlier examples of ballet partnering that often developed in service of furthering the narrative

The Prince and Odette in the iconic white swan pas de deux from *Swan Lake*.
Robbie Jack/Corbis via Getty Images

libretto of ballet and opera performances, a noted codification came in the form of Petipa's grand pas de deux. With prescribed sections and a formulaic structure, Petipa's grand pas became the gold standard in most of the ballets created thereafter.

The sociocultural and political climate of a time and place also affected the outcomes seen onstage. With most independent and opera-affiliated ballet companies in Europe supported by their nation's government (largely funded by taxes paid by citizens), social politics held substantial sway over the arts of that time. In *The Male Dancer*, Ramsay Burt explains a notable example from the Victorian age. Within the romantic period of ballet in Western Europe, negative attitudes emerged regarding the image of dancing men, such that they were eliminated from ballets in England, France, Italy, and Spain and were replaced with female dancers performing male roles *en traviste*, or in male dress (Burt 2007). Two main exceptions were the ballet companies of the Imperial Russian court and the ballets of August Bournonville (1805-1879) of Denmark. Russia's cultural standards and restrictions of that time did not lead to the exclusion of male dancers from their ballets, and Bournonville's narrative focus on less monarchical and aristocratic protagonists (e.g., James in *La Sylphide*, a farmer and landowner rather than a prince or god) seemed to insulate his dancing men from such critiques. Bournonville's unique style was highly influenced by regional, culturally specific dances but also maintained a requisite amount of athleticism and masculine drive that seemed to make male dancing more palatable to his audiences (Christensen 2007).

As time passed, the codified techniques and forms in ballet remained much the same. In the early and mid-20th century, choreographers such as Frederick Ashton (1904-1988) and George Balanchine (1904-1983) pushed ballet toward neoclassicism with a more modernist style. For example, Balanchine moved away from the narrative form and was heavily influenced by African diasporic and American vernacular dance forms. His style focused primarily on the movement itself and its close relationship with musical expression. Like his technique and movement aesthetic, Balanchine's approach to choreographing partnering within his ballets also pushed beyond what was expected (or previously acceptable) within ballet vocabulary. Classical ballet's tendency toward slow development and a staunch maintenance of traditions and standards within a highly codified system of movement vocabulary led to the reproduction of a seemingly unequal power dynamic within ballet partnering. The primary role of the male dancer in pas de deux was to support, lift, frame, and focus the attention on his partner; the ballerina's role was to accept support and present her own technical excellence, elegance, and ethereal beauty while maintaining a sense of effortlessness and ease. Consider the following point from Burt in *The Male Dancer*:

> It would be simplistic to dismiss ballet pas de deux in general as no more than an exhibition in which the female dancer is an object to be manipulated. Duets signify social relations. The actual practice of partnering and lifting is one which requires a high degree of skill and cooperation between the male and female dancer. (Burt 2007, 46)

Although the cooperative, mutual dynamic present in the technique of ballet's pas de deux is clear to those well versed in dance, classical ballet's aesthetic of (seemingly) effortless, ethereal grace for its ballerinas seems (to the untrained eye) to be an imbalance of physical labor and agency. Contemporary and neoclassical approaches that shifted the ballerina's role away from narrative and character-specific performativity opened a broader range of movement vocabulary and made the mutuality of ballet partnering more evident. Closely related to these newer aesthetics in ballet, partnering in the modernist movement in dance that followed maintained more of the individual agency that developed between partners.

## Modern Dance

George Balanchine's inventions and innovations within the ballet idiom developed along-side the pioneers of early modernism and shared a number of its efforts to move away from the strict constraints of classicism. Unique to the development of modern dance is the fact that most of its earliest leaders were women (Burt 2007). Although ballet in the early 20th century also saw an increase in female leadership, particularly in Britain, with Marie Rambert (1888-1982) and Ninette de Valois (1898-2001), men occupied most exec-utive and artistic management roles in ballet companies. Burt explains it was clear that "one reason why women initially developed a new area—modern dance—was because of their restricted access to creative positions in the existing one" (Burt 2007, 3).

The earliest American modern dances of Loïe Fuller (1862-1928), Isadora Duncan (1877-1927), and Ruth St. Denis (1879-1968) often centered soloists and ensemble group work to express and exalt the individual and collective power and artistry of women depicted through their own lens. Similarly, Ted Shawn (1891-1972) and his male dancers used the liberated movement potential of modern dance to depict the strength, vigor, and prowess of a collective of dancing men. For the most part, the first generation of modern dance choreographers focused almost entirely on ensemble group forms, with movement vocab-ularies developed and codified based on their own unique ways of moving.

Doris Humphrey (1895-1958) was a notable exception. In an explanation of this dynamic in *Dancing Women: Female Bodies on Stage*, Sally Banes points out that "unlike Mary Wigman, Martha Graham, Hanya Holm, and other choreographers of her generation who formed all-female dance groups, Humphrey had consciously chosen to work with a

Charles Weidman and Doris Humphrey in *Duo-Drama* (1935).

Jerome Robbins Dance Division, The New York Public Library for the Performing Arts, Astor, Lenox and Tilden Foundations

gender-integrated group, co-directed by male colleague, Charles Weidman" (Banes 1998, 136). Graham later shifted toward greater use of partnering when an interest in dramatic narrative as a framework for her artistic and aesthetic communication necessitated the inclusion of male dancers. Although they still held lesser featured roles within her dances, men became more integrated into the landscape of Graham's repertoire. With the role of Jocasta in *Night Journey* (1947), Graham included a featured role for her first male dance partner and husband to be, Erick Hawkins (1909-1994), as her husband and son, Oedipus. Although much of Graham's work expresses the power and autonomy of women, the interaction with male partners often undermined that overarching effort within her dances when the narrative dictated a different dynamic. Banes points to both *Night Journey* and the earlier *Appalachian Spring* (1944) to discuss this dichotomy:

> In both dances, the woman often becomes passive and immobile when touched by her man. He may lift or carry her, but when he does so, unlike in classical ballet, his support rarely helps her to fly or to take movement risks . . . she is most open, most luxuriating in space when she dances alone. (Banes 1998, 163-164)

A look to the next generation in the creative lineage of modern dance reveals even more unique, balanced, and original uses of dance partnering. The second generation was removed from the initial rebelliousness (to ballet) of the early modern dance period; thus, it focused on other endeavors and dynamics and perhaps more directly reflects that place and time, leaving behind the myths and legends of the past.

For many innovators of early modern dance, the process of rejecting and moving away from the creative constraints of ballet and the often-restrictive boundary on female leadership led them to seek inspiration elsewhere. St. Denis and Graham are well known for overt and heavy influences by global dance forms. Graham looked often to the myths and legends of ancient Greece and Rome and the artistic and aesthetic frames of global forms, although her movement vocabulary was narrow in specificity and scope as she developed her codified technique and performative style. By contrast, St. Denis would often directly appropriate historical and culturally specific dances from around the world and reperform them in choreographed vignettes that served almost as exhibitions of the global styles. Although modern understanding of cultural appropriation recognizes the problematic nature of white artists capitalizing on the commodification of global dance forms, it is worth noting that interest in global dance was originally based on curiosity about how else humans might move, express, and artistically communicate through dance.

Nonwhite artists in the early modern period with modern dance approaches significantly drawn from their personal histories within African diasporic and Caribbean dance forms, such as Pearl Primus (1919-1994) and later Katherine Dunham (1909-2006), are often overlooked when the genesis and evolution of modern dance is considered. These women, along with contemporaries such as Talley Beatty (1918-1995), Donald McKayle (1930-2018), and Alvin Ailey (1931-1989), made significant contributions to the greater modern dance field and also paved the way for many artists of color. Following in their footsteps and after their example, many dance makers have engaged in impactful and powerful artistic and intellectual considerations of identity, diversity, and representation within the field.

The influence and appropriation of the many dance forms with global roots cannot be overlooked when one considers the complexity of lineage within the broad field of modern (and contemporary) dance. Since the founders of the form were uniformly interested in learning and inflecting their own movement and artistry with traces of global dance, this lineage within the body, mind, and spirit of dancers today cannot be denied. Dance

Ruth St. Denis and Ted Shawn in Dance of the Rebirth from *Egyptian Suite* (1917).

Jerome Robbins Dance Division, The New York Public Library for the Performing Arts, Astor, Lenox and Tilden Foundations.

practices from the African diaspora, Caribbean, Central and South America, and East and South Asia have significantly influenced modern and contemporary dance. Although social dance and ballroom dance are not studied in depth in this book, these forms were highly influenced by the transatlantic cultural exchange and appropriation between Europe, Africa, and North, Central, and South America, with dance often functioning as a national export.

In *The Body Eclectic*, Melanie Bales frames the hybridity common to recent and current dance training as *bricolage*. Officially defined as construction or creation from a diverse range of available things, bricolage in dance training can easily define the overlap in training approaches, influence and evolution rooted in global forms, and blending of aesthetics, techniques, and qualities of style. Bales frames this in contrast with the set, codified techniques and styles of modern dance, which held tighter borders to maintain tight movement vocabularies and aesthetic and dramatic value (Bales and Nettl-Fiol 2008). Bales frames dance training as both constructive (building up technique, skills, and artistry with an additive approach) and deconstructive (stripping back affectation and habitual movement pathways to produce a more neutral technical base). As in the Judson Dance Group's work and much of the postmodern era in dance broadly, Bales asserts that "the initial step of *rejecting* [emphasis mine] is followed by a phase of selective choice" in stripping back (Bales and Nettl-Fiol 2008, 36).

## Postmodern Dance

The 1960s were marked by political activism, including antiwar protests and movements for civil rights and racial equality, women's liberation, and LGBTQ+ rights. The United States was changing—fast. A younger, bolder generation sought to stand up for their political beliefs and make their voices heard. This transformational energy was alive within the arts world as well; experimentation became common in nearly every performing and visual art form. The social unrest and rebellious youth energy that epitomized the U.S. cultural climate of the 1960s was fertile ground for the growth of political, social, and cultural reforms in the arts and a catalyst for questioning gender and performance within the field.

Broadly speaking, postmodernism in dance shared the overarching goal of rejecting the traditions and values of modern dance. Although hindsight reveals somewhat shared borders of time and creative approaches, each artist had an approach to the process of rejection and the selective choice that followed. Innovation and experimentation became touchstones for postmodern dance, as did a collective turn toward pedestrian movement and performance aesthetics rooted in a desire for greater inclusion, community building, rejection of hierarchies, and an anti-illusionism that opposed the dramatic narrative and fanciful representation of the modern dance period.

Often attributed to the experimentation of the downtown scene in New York dance circles, the Judson Dance Group and the Grand Union emerged as a sort of center of gravity for this shift in style, aesthetics, and technical approach. At the same time, Anna Halprin (1920-2021) and Simone Forti (1935-) led the postmodern turn on the American West Coast. Both women embraced the performative use of improvisation and radical inclusion of dancers and nondancers alike in performance events and happenings. Their creative practice and theoretical engagement through dance making and training dovetailed with the general rejection of the ego-based, choreographer-is-king framework of modern dance, with its codified systems based on famous individuals. Merce Cunningham (1919-2009) and John Cage's (1912-1992) experimentations with chance procedures, Halprin and Forti's use of improvisation and community inclusion, and the innovative developments coming out of the Judson Church in American dance in the 1960s and 1970s all stemmed from the desire to decenter the artist from the conversation as the all-knowing genius or guru of dance. In *Terpsichore in Sneakers: Post-Modern Dance*, Sally Banes deftly sums up the aim of the time:

> Originally acting against the expressionism of modern dance, which anchored movement to a literary idea or musical form, the postmodernists propose (as do Cunningham and Balanchine) that the formal qualities of dance might be reason enough for choreography, and that the purpose of making dances might be simply to make a framework within which we look at movement for its own sake. (Banes 1987, 15)

Banes' isolation of Cunningham and Balanchine stems from her arguments that the creative philosophies and methodologies of these influential choreographers were in line with postmodern thinking, but their maintenance of formalist composition and their highly technical movement vocabularies set them apart from the more pedestrian aesthetics of the time. Taken in proportion, Balanchine's movement inventions, rejection of narrative, and simple, nonrepresentational costume and scenic approach within most of his dances constitute a radical shift from the restrictions of classical ballet. Cunningham's philosophical, theoretical, and radical approach to dance composition also flew in the face of modern dance's guru culture. His aesthetic simplicity also aligned more closely with the ethos of the postmodern movement than with the approaches of his mentors.

*RainForest* (1968), choreographed by Merce Cunningham.
Jack Mitchell/Getty Images

While many aesthetic, methodological, and philosophical changes were underway in the postmodern dance period, the partnering approach in choreographed work continued to draw from the techniques and mechanics of ballet and modern dance. Although a large shift toward improvisation yielded more risk and experimentation in partnered interactions, the development of contact improvisation by Steve Paxton (1939-) and his collaborators proved to be the most significant shift in the approach to partnering that would continue into contemporary dance approaches from the 1980s onward.

## Contact Improvisation

Contact improvisation was developed in the mid-1960s primarily by Steve Paxton, along with Nancy Stark Smith (1952-2020) and various students who aided in several residencies and workshops. The most famous of these and often credited as the genesis of contact improvisation was a workshop offered at Oberlin College during a tour by the Grand Union, of which Paxton was a member and collaborator. In line with the overall thrust of the postmodern movement in dance, which focused on providing dance training access to anyone through an inclusive and anti-elitist effort, contact improvisation was imagined as a form of partnering that did not require brute strength or years of training and removed gender as a prerequisite for participation in the duet form.

With its unique, egalitarian, and ungendered nature, contact improvisation had a significant influence on social and cultural outlooks that few other dance forms have matched. By challenging the status quo, self-critical focus and rule-breaking quickly became the signs of the time. Steve Paxton's contact improvisation emerged at the beginning of the 1970s, carrying with it many sociopolitical concerns of the 1960s. Like many art forms linked to cultural concerns, contact improvisation was a product of 1960s and 1970s culture and society. In *Sharing the Dance*, an ethnographic study of contact improvisation as it relates to American culture, Cynthia J. Novack writes that the form "demonstrates how dance is a part of life and culture—as a metaphor for social interaction and values . . . as the direct apprehension of moving with and for a community of people" (Novack 1990, 235).

The very nature of contact improvisation dictates that it is a product of the whole group's efforts, not a singular creation of one individual. Despite Paxton's discomfort with being hailed as the father and guru of contact improvisation, he continually emphasized his desire for the form to uphold the values of "egalitarianism and communality" that were characteristic of the members of the Judson Dance Group (Novack 1990, 235). The *contact jam*, or the communal framework for both the practice and performance of contact improvisation, creates the open, inclusive environment for which the dance form is known. As a partnered form, contact improvisation cannot be danced alone and thus relies on the presence of community to engage in its practice.

Contact improvisation can also be credited for significant advancements in the politics of gender and sex, both societally and within the field of dance. Drawing from her experiences within the contact improvisation community, Novack notes the general feeling that "the movement structure of contact improvisation literally embodied the social ideologies of the early '70s which rejected traditional gender roles and social hierarchies" (Novack 1990, 11). The sensual nature of the form allowed for any combination of gendered pairs to have a truly intimate, physical interaction removed from overt sexual intention. Functional concerns of ability relating to a particular gender were also eliminated by the framework of the improvisatory nature of the form. Contact improvisation is essentially the outcome of a simple duet score: fall, spill, press into, and ride a maintained point of contact with another dancer. Various techniques, skills, and mechanics have developed from the practice of contact improvisation over many years, but an understanding of its simple score—coupled with an open and willing mind and body—is all that is required to begin practicing.

What emerged from the framework created by Paxton's ideas and resulting from his work with the initial groups that helped to unearth and realize the form was a dance that did not require a particular degree of strength, stability, or power. Thus, contact improvisation operated outside the concerns of gender for participation. Anyone could, should, or would dance with anyone, regardless of biological sex. The outcome of dancing a contact improvisation duet with another body was easily framed in relation to the abilities of each dancer. The dance resulting from a particular pairing was as physically and visually varied as the participants involved; this was a source of great pride for the dance form's originators and practitioners. Both technically and philosophically, the egalitarian dynamic of contact improvisation upheld the utopian values of the contact community as well as those of the larger postmodern dance culture from which it emerged and operated within.

In the simplest terms, contact improvisation explorations are predicated on two individuals connecting their centers of gravity at a single point of contact, with varying degrees of weight sharing. The partners' task is to continuously fall into that shared point of contact by maintaining malleability in their legs to accommodate any shift in motion or flow while engaging other zones of the body. In contact improvisation, the mutual, 50-50 nature of weight sharing is driven by the form's initial theoretical and physical ideals related to egalitarian interaction and nonhierarchical dynamics between partners. Therefore, the practice serves as a wonderful bridge toward exercises and choreographed phrases that require increased responsibility for support and weight in less equal measure.

## Contemporary Dance

Contemporary dance is less overtly defined because it continues to evolve, and many qualities of current approaches to dance training and dance making move beyond modern and postmodern dance values and styles. As Melanie Bales points to hybridity and bricolage, contemporary dance practice can be considered as a true amalgamation of many combinations of dance styles, techniques, and aesthetics depending on the approach. Contemporary dance practice from the late 1980s (perhaps a post-postmodern or post-Judson era?) into the 21st century and today is marked by a broad integration and confluence of multiple styles. The reincorporation of ballet technique, jazz, hip-hop, street dance, and global forms and more contemporary approaches to dance technique and performance are marked by interest in versatility, diversity, and collaborative, integrative approaches.

Between the broadening of technical training and performative styles, the current period of artistic and creative development in dance is clearly marked by an embrace of the spectrum of what is possible. The multifaceted, interdisciplinary approaches of many current dance practitioners point to open-ended potential for future directions of the dance field.

It is important to note that in academic, theoretical, and historical contexts, the term *contemporary* has been widely contested, often to the point of contradiction. In the context of this book, contemporary mostly refers to a marker of time or temporal category. The aesthetics and style of contemporary concert dance are also referenced in later chapters, primarily reflecting the hybrid, varied aesthetics mentioned above. In her article "When Is Contemporary Dance?," SanSan Kwan brilliantly outlines the complexities of the use and understanding of the term contemporary in the dance field. She explains that "the term 'contemporary dance' is fraught and contended across dance genres. It does not mean the same thing in all dance communities" (Kwan 2017, 39). She articulates that, as an aesthetic term pointing to style, contemporary varies greatly whether in the context of concert dance, commercial dance, or world dance forms.

The current moment in the field of dance is complex. Dance is in a period of flux—a flux of invention and reinvention, historical preservation, and possibility. However, social and cultural shifts toward technology, shorter attention spans, and commercial commodification of culture do not bode well for the continuation of a rich and deeply investigated version of this art form. By working outside of definitions and narrow frameworks, dancers might burst the seams of creative possibility and return to efforts grounded in exploration, innovation, and creative freedom.

## Historical Contexts in Practice

Where do readers go from here? As the following chapters move into the practical and technical aspects of dance partnering, readers can carry the historical contexts described here into that work. Although the mechanical aspects of partnering certainly merit emphasis, consideration of the social, political, and cultural roots of its origins and development can foster deeper and more meaningful exploration within dance practices broadly and dance partnering contexts specifically.

The chapters that follow apply the lenses of curriculum building and class planning, cross-training and body awareness, creative practice and improvisation, and community building and inclusive pedagogy to the practice of dance partnering. Partnering informed by the confluence of ballet partnering, modern and contemporary partnering, and contact improvisation is the primary focus of this foundational approach; as such, social dance and ballroom forms are not covered significantly. The nuance of touch, yielding of weight, sense of risk, and accessing of momentum are attributes gleaned from the study of contact improvisation. Clarity, mechanics, balance, and exactitude, along with dedicated practice using leverage, vertical momentum, and coordination, are drawn from consideration of the technical underpinnings of ballet and modern partnering. Contemporary partnering offers off-center, nonverbal, and unique aspects of dance partnering and incorporates more direct contact between bodies and both touch and support that go beyond work at arm's length. A look at these contemporary approaches and the confluence of forms within an integrated practice then moves readers toward creative development of partnering within choreographic practice and improvisatory process and performance.

## SUMMARY

While the historical overview offered in this chapter is by no means exhaustive, the intention is to trace the lineages and distinct practices that are referenced in the practical approaches with the book in order to offer context and the potential for integration as a rounded understanding of a range of useful techniques and mechanics within dance partnering. The utilization of key elements drawn from ballet, modern and contemporary dance partnering, contact improvisation, and even ballroom and social dance, foster a broad understanding of dance partnering trainings.

Chapter 2, Time: Getting Started, considers the planning and curricular design of dance partnering education experiences from both macro and micro perspectives to help the educator identify a place to begin. Frameworks for individual application of the techniques included in the text are offered to allow the reader to customize a plan for their particular population of students. The first group of Practical Exercises 1-7 are introduced in the second half of the chapter via Practical Skills and Frameworks for Teaching Dance Partnering: Part I.

## DISCUSSION QUESTIONS

1. What dance styles, genres, or practices have contributed to your own dancing history?
2. Is there a technique that has become the central foundation of your approach to dance?
3. What styles have you studied that have diversified your perspective or relationship to dance technique?
4. What role has partnering played in your personal dance journey?

Niki Powell and Sky Pasqual in *HER* (abridged). Santa Barbara Dance Theater. Choreography by Brandon Whited.

© Fritz Olenberger

# 2

# TIME: Getting Started

## OVERVIEW

This chapter taps into broad frameworks of skill building in dance partnering and offers specific exercises to build the foundational tools necessary for continued practice and entry into more in-depth partnered work. The sample topical outlines for semester or quarter arcs, daily lesson plans, and individual exercises in this chapter take broad curricular considerations and turn them into ideas for daily practice. These exercises may also inspire framing for individualized instructor pedagogical approaches and styles.

### VOCABULARY

| | |
|---|---|
| base of support | durational support |
| center of gravity | plumb line |
| contact improvisation | point of contact |
| counterbalance | weight sharing |

This chapter considers how instructors might plan for and organize the dance partnering exercises that follow. The Key Concepts section outlines skills, values, and outcomes in dance partnering training and can serve as a template for teaching practice. The Developing Curriculum section offers a blueprint for planning a single semester or quarter dance partnering course from an multimodal perspective that introduces broad aspects of multiple forms. Instructors may emphasize one form over others or create a course that focuses on one genre. The Planning Classes section reviews planning the flow of an individual class, workshop, or master class. Individual exercises can be grouped to provide building blocks supporting a particular phrase of partnering material or to link concepts leading to a movement sequence drawn from the exercises. Finally, part I of the three-part Practical Skills and Frameworks for Teaching Dance Partnering series presents a foundation of comfort and confidence on which to build more complex exercises.

Planning a dance partnering class can be overwhelming. Educators and creators may ponder questions like these: Where does the foundation for partnering training begin on a curricular level? What should I consider when designing a contemporary partnering class? What should I consider while building an arc for a full semester or quarter? How can students embrace, apply, and synthesize the practical skills associated with dance partnering? Start by sharing with students the core benefits, freedoms, and connections unique to dance partnering. Transparent communication of the function and purpose of the exercises and explorations offered in classes or rehearsal settings can calm anxiety, apprehension, and vulnerability among students new to partnering. This chapter describes how to provide foundational skills to facilitate meaningful, safe, and engaging partnered experiences within varied training environments.

## Key Concepts: Contents of Training and Objectives in Dance Partnering

It is helpful to define the overarching goals, methods, content, and expected outcomes for students as they begin a practice. The following broader skills, dynamics, and techniques are goals for and benefits of a rounded study of dance partnering:

- *Basic skills and fundamentals:* weight sharing, counterbalance, weight-bearing and mechanics of support, and perching and shelving
- *Interpersonal awareness:* sensitivity, cooperation, communication (verbal and physical), trust and safety, and attention to and knowledge of a partner's role, movement, and needs
- *Technique and mechanics:* coordination, timing, follow-through, conditioning, strengthening, cross-training, and development of deep core stabilization and efficient weight transfer
- *Learning to listen:* problem-solving and cooperation, physical listening and awareness, and development of body care, body work, and safe practices
- *Dynamics of touch:* degrees and qualitative range of touch (superficial and deep), weight and sensitivity, and sensing, patience, listening, and breath
- *Politics of touch:* identification of nuanced approaches to touch and connection, safety and consent in the partnering classroom, dynamics of teacher-to-student versus student-to-student touch, religious and cultural restrictions and considerations, and sensitivity as a response to trauma
- *Momentum and energy:* stabilization and mobilization, and accessing and using momentum, leverage, flow, and drive

- *Nuance and patterning:* familiar and nontraditional points of contact, phrasing and musicality, and understanding and employing safe mechanics for efficiency
- *Creative exploration:* partnering emerging through movement generation and composition (time, space, and energy) and creating prompts for improvisational, in-the-moment choice making

The instructor's goals for students may expand on or differ from those expressed here. These key concepts might then be used to guide and frame course planning filtered through the individualized lens of the instructor.

# Developing Curriculum

There are many considerations related to developing curriculum, and their scale and scope depend on the circumstances of instruction. It would be misguided to discuss models for curriculum building related to a series of dance partnering courses, given that many dance programs, studios, and organizations do not have a robust partnering training practice. Consider how the inclusion of a dance partnering course may fit with other course offerings. How can dance partnering relate to, support, and expand on other training methods? For this introductory consideration of dance partnering pedagogy, curriculum development as described next relates to course planning or similar applications within a series of workshops.

## Zooming Out: Semester or Quarter Planning

First, zoom out to broad principles for consideration when planning a dance partnering curriculum. Although instructor needs may differ based on the educational and social settings, the broad principles introduced here provide a framework that can be tailored. How might the instructor maximize the instruction within a single course or, given the opportunity, create a series of partnering classes that build on one another and allow advanced students to deepen their practice? This section offers models for a 10-week program. The next section covers an individual master class, but can of course be tailored to suit individual program needs.

The following pages present sample topical outlines to illustrate different organizational approaches to planning a series of partnering classes, with the aim to build a foundational skill set or tool kit. These outlines provide specific course plans that can be used as offered or can serve as inspiration for reinterpretation and personalization. Table 2.1 presents the author's Integrated Partnering course, a 10-week sequence designed for the quarter system. Both the class format and pace are designed to survey multiple partnering genres—contact improvisation, ballet, and contemporary partnering—to help students understand the many intersections of the seemingly different forms. Within a longer, semester-based version, ballroom dance and social dance are also offered.

## Topical Outline: Integrated Partnering

A topical outline can be broad or detailed. A broad outline focuses on the overarching genres and principles to be explored in a given week, which allows students to prepare mentally for what is to come and to have a clearer sense of what to expect. This outline then becomes a broad guide for the instructor to plan, organize, and manage their individual class plans and the overall flow of the course. A detailed outline may include the specific skills or exercises to be taught. Keeping the details broad allows for more flux in plan implementation; the instructor has more room to stay on a topic or move on quickly depending on student needs and interests.

**TABLE 2.1**    Integrated Partnering Course: 10-Week Topical Outline

| Week of instruction | Topic of instruction and genre of practice | Detailed focus and class content |
|---|---|---|
| Week 1 | Introduction: weight basics | Syllabus overview and ice breakers; weight exploration or partnered body work |
| Week 2 | Connecting: foundations | Weight sharing, counterbalance, and perch or self-support |
| Week 3 | Contact improvisation | Introduction to more advanced contact improvisation principles |
| Week 4 | Ballet partnering: skills | Traditional partnering skills, support, and mechanics |
| Week 5 | Ballet partnering: application or repertory | Phrase work building on traditional partnering principles |
| Week 6 | Ballet partnering: contemporary partnering | Bridging genres; relating shared mechanics and skills |
| Week 7 | Contemporary partnering | Phrase work and repertory selections |
| Week 8 | Contemporary partnering | Sustained and durational support in partnering |
| Week 9 | Collaboration, composition, and improvisation | Skills in the process for movement development |
| Week 10 | Collaboration, composition, and improvisation | **Final:** presentation of collaborative compositions |

From B. Whited, *Dance Partnering Basics: Practical Skills and Inclusive Pedagogy.* (Champaign, IL: Human Kinetics, 2025).

## Weeks 1 Through 3

In weeks 1 through 3, use low-risk, low-weight-bearing exercises to develop trust. Doing so allows students to test their confidence and comfort level while the stakes are lower. Even dancers who are familiar with their classmates but new to partnering may feel like they must become reacquainted. In partnering training, students are asked to go beyond social dynamics and friendly relatability to a place of trust, reliability, strength, and physical connection. Momentum and risk are exciting dynamics when prepared for and used appropriately, but encouraging sensitivity is a vital step toward confident and safe exploration of deeper progressions. Experienced partners can also benefit, because this progression allows them to adapt to and connect with their peers. For advanced students, the learning process may be quicker, but there is significant benefit to beginning with less risk and more nuance even within a single class or short workshop series.

Approaches rooted in contact improvisation (detailed in chapter 1) are introduced as the course progresses. In contact improvisation, the mutual, 50-50 nature of weight sharing is driven by its initial theoretical and physical ideals related to egalitarian interaction and nonhierarchical dynamics between partners (Novack 1990). Because of this emphasis on balance and equity, contact improvisation is a wonderful bridge toward exercises and choreographed phrases that require the dynamic of supporting and giving weight equally. Improvisation also allows for varying degrees of risk, play, and exploration, because students can decide to share less weight, slow their practice, or simplify exploration until they become more comfortable. This mitigation gives both instructors and students time to assess readiness and build trust and confidence. To illustrate the sense of release and falling that contact improvisation requires, use a yoga or exercise ball to stand in as students' first partner.

## ▶ YOGA BALL AS PARTNER

Student using a Yoga ball as a partner to build toward risk and momentum in contact improvisation.

Surfing practice (i.e., giving weight with momentum) using a yoga ball as a partner allows students to feel full release and ride momentum before they work with others.

▶ PARTNERED SURFING EXERCISE

Preparation for contact improvisation, and follow-up to Yoga ball exploration.

### Weeks 4 Through 6

Ballet partnering is explored at arm's length in weeks 4 through 6. Distal connections (hand partnering), formality, and presentation of the supported partner are common in ballet, in which nuanced degrees of distance are maintained between partners and body-to-body contact is minimized (Serebrennikov 2000). With its emphasis on strength, timing, leverage, and plumb line awareness, there is much to learn from ballet even if this form is not central to the curriculum. Teaching ballet partnering in a nongendered way, with both individuals working equally and trading roles, offers a balanced understanding of a somewhat imbalanced form (relative to its use of traditional roles). Practicing the mechanics, timing, nuanced musicality, balance clarity, and gravity defiance of ballet partnering also offers an exciting and strength-building experience for students. As in similar approaches to teaching social dance and ballroom classes in which all students learn to both lead and follow, this ballet partnering approach naturally fosters a more inclusive space for students. For excellent examples of this type of learning, see exercise 14, Promenade, and exercise 15, Traditional Lifts, in chapter 4. For further reading on ballet partnering, see the second edition of *Pas de Deux: A Textbook on Partnering* by Nikolai Serebrennikov (2000).

### Weeks 7 Through 9

In weeks 7 through 9, the mechanics learned in the ballet-focused unit, coupled with understanding of weight, flow, and bodily connections gained from early foundational work and contact improvisation, allow for more confident entry into the complex, hybrid approaches characteristic of contemporary partnering. Students employ strength, timing, leverage, and momentum, along with nuance and sensitivity to touch and weight. Use of body architecture, alternative partnered connections beyond hand use, and comfort with moving in and out of the ground all come into play when exploring contemporary repertory, improvisational partnering, and development of partnering in students' creative, choreographic work.

### Week 10

To conclude this teaching arc, week 10 centers on collaborative student projects that use the skills and techniques learned over the quarter. Weather permitting, site-specific framing that allows time outside can be a welcome change of scenery from the studio. Studio-based projects are equally as effective in the distillation of material learned within the course and students' application of the collaboration, cooperation, and communication skills developed. Invited showings of students' final projects, performances, presentations on their process, and discussions are excellent ways to wrap up the partnering learning experience. Student reflection on their progress can also meaningfully wrap up their hard work over many weeks. *How did I do? What did I learn? What improved, and what would I still like to work on? What fears and inhibitions did I release through this practice?*

Note that this shortened topical outline does not include a dedicated study of social dance, ballroom partnering, or folk-dance forms. The skills in the trainings here develop a strong sense of frame, nonverbal communication, posture, and non-weight-bearing cooperation, all of which dovetail nicely with ballet, modern, and contemporary partnering. For the 10-week quarter system, this social dance learning unit is removed to tighten the flow and allow adequate time for more directly related techniques. With more time (e.g., over a semester or multiple quarters), partnering techniques in social and ballroom dance can be explored to further enrich the student experience.

# Planning Classes

Although curriculum planning is often complex and broad, the crafting of individual classes in a sequence or one-off master classes offered by a guest instructor can be equally meaningful for students. I fondly remember certain classes that felt transcendent and special, and thoughtful planning can foster such an outcome. The following master class plan provides warm-up progressions and exercises, building toward phrase work or choreography that engages the principles learned within the chosen movement explorations. (For more sample class plans and different exercise combinations, see the Sample Class Plans section in HK*Propel*.)

## Zooming In: The Master Class

In studio environments and within higher education, a master class can provide an opportunity for students to dive into new styles and approaches to dance. Classes dedicated to the study of partnering benefit preprofessional students, who often work within stressful rehearsal environments in which learning choreography quickly is essential. By exposing students to foundational partnered explorations and exercises, they can gain the confidence, coordination, and interpersonal skills necessary for safe and rewarding partnered experiences.

A common pitfall of planning for a one-off master class (or even a short series of classes in a guest engagement) is overplanning and attempting to fit too much into a short time frame. Although it can help to prepare for the rare occasion that a class progresses quicker than expected, leaving space for the exploration, discussion, and workshopping of concepts can be beneficial for students within this singular experience. Educators are often eager to share as much experience and knowledge as possible; however, a well-planned, manageable, and tightly curated master class experience can do even more for students' depth of learning.

The following sections outline how to approach a master class focused on the introductory fundamentals of dance partnering. This outline is based on contributing author Joshua Manculich's 60- to 90-minute Contemporary Partnering master class, which is geared toward preprofessional dancers aged 13 to 18 years. Both the class format and pace (1) showcase the need for partnering and (2) embody fundamental partnering explorations that prepare the dancer for the rehearsal and new creative processes. Although classes do not all need to progress to phrase work or choreography, students often revel in sinking their teeth into a memorable phrase to anchor the learned skills in a set sequence of movement. The instructor can save time and increase confidence by using the exercises and explorations of particular skills as the building blocks of the culminating phrase, since students will have already had the chance to understand the principles used in the material. A reverse approach is also particularly useful: If the instructor has existing duet phrase or section of a longer piece of choreography, they can identify the techniques and mechanics used in the phrase and plan a few exercises that will prepare students for that material. In this way, the instructor might plan the class to serve the phrase as a place to begin.

### Opening Remarks: Providing Context

In a master class in contemporary partnering, it is important to first connect with and hear from students. In many dance studio classroom settings, students welcome the need for instruction in contemporary partnering and may have questions and topics for discussion. To increase your understanding of students' experience and direct their curiosity, ask questions like these:

1. Where have you experienced contemporary partnering?
2. What skills are required in contemporary partnering?
3. How do we approach partnering in choreography? In rehearsal?

### Warm-Up: Drawing Connections

Getting students to embody new tasks requires a warm-up that integrates the upper and lower body. Ideally, an instructor-led improvisation focused on space and sensing one another can also benefit students in a full-body warm-up. The instructor can also provide affirmation and encouragement by reminding students that they already practice and understand the core principles needed for partnered work. See chapter 3 for more detailed suggestions for warm-up progressions. Some individual exercises include suggestions for guided improvisations that help students prepare for the exercises to come.

Examples of warm-ups include the following:

1. A cardiovascular sequence and improvisation may ask dancers to fill up the space within the room while considering teacher-guided tasks and prompts. Maintaining for three to five minutes can raise the heart rate and warm the body.
2. In a typical dance warm-up combination, the instructor highlights and emphasizes the aspects that support partnering technique and also explains that partnering extends students' prior individual training. Breath, weight sensing, weight transfer, flow, and awareness of the body in space are principles that students may be familiar with and can be used within the lens of partnering.

### Organize

Because of the time constraints of master class settings, lining students up by height can be a reliable way to organize which students might be best suited to partner with each other. Explain that for the master class, this arrangement is necessary for safety and efficiency. Reinforce that students should forge new partnerships within continued explorations and partnering training and that the opportunity to dance and work with a range of partners is vital to studying dance partnering.

### Explore: Explain Movement Concepts

Within a single master class, instructors are limited in how much they can cover coherently. Time management in these settings is key. Aim to use exercises to ground the key partnering concepts that will be covered. Doing so maintains a workshop environment in which the instructor shares in exploration and discovery with students, rather than leaning into a more lecture-based mode of instruction. By framing and verbalizing concepts in a series of exercises, a beginning partnering student has access to ways of problem-solving and igniting their own creative approach, which are required for final culminating combinations or phrase work. The following progression example explores and provides instruction on proper and safe hand use, in which the instructor introduces touch in a way that allows students to acclimate quicker but without the addition of weight at first. The class then progresses to exploration or weight sharing and counterbalance (its opposite) and introduces the supportive potential of shelves and ledges. Here is a potential sequence: exercise 1, Grasp and Clasp; exercise 4, Weight Sharing; exercise 5, Counterbalance; and exercise 6, Shelves and Ledges.

## Linking

The class culminates by linking the explored skills (exercises 1, 4, 5, and 6) in a final phrase of material. In this way, students are exposed to movement principles and skills incrementally and observe that the techniques can then be translated into a dance by adding specificity, nuanced timing, and smooth and intentional transitions between movements. If students have varied experience, offer modifications within the phrase so they can enjoy the full experience without being mired in advanced skills.

# Alternative Examples of Individual Class Plans

Numerous combinations of the exercises in this book and other sources center a specific technique or skill set within partnering. Individual class plans that use combinations of exercises are offered next, which can serve as a springboard for class plans. Refer to the written instructions for individual exercises and the linked videos and photos for full explanations and suggestions.

## Introduction to Contact Improvisation

In this individual class plan, start with the warm-up and then move on to the exercises as described.

**Warm-Up**
Guide dancers through exercise 3, Active and Passive, to reintroduce this low-risk weight-bearing exercise. Work from one student being the active partner and the other following as the passive partner. After a few minutes and a change of roles, students begin again and shift between the active and passive roles within one exploration.

**Exercises**

- Exercise 4, Weight Sharing, allows students to explore lowering into and rising from the floor. Student pairs begin with equal weight and then explore adding and subtracting weight to mobilize the pair.
- Exercise 6, Shelves and Ledges, encourages students to locate and activate potential moments for small lifts and full support of their partner.
- Try the yoga ball exploration. Students explore pouring and releasing their weight into a yoga ball by using the pull and push of their arms and legs into the floor to surf, roll, and slide in and out of the support of the ball. This is a safe way to explore the sense of falling into a point of contact, which is central to the practice of contact improvisation. If yoga balls are not available, practicing falling and spilling into the ground, with or without the use of mats, can also be a useful exploration prior to engaging a partner.

**Final Exploration: Round-Robin Improvisation**
Once students have explored some of these exercises in pairs during class, use the last 10 to 15 minutes to organize the whole group in a wide open circle. Invite students to enter or exit the dancing space inside the circle at any point. They begin by improvising alone and can find partners in or entering the circle to explore contact improvisation based on the principles learned in class.

## Ballet Partnering

This class plan starts with a warm-up and then continues with the exercises.

**Warm-Up**

Use a short barre warm-up with brief exercises focused on accessing vertical balance and activating the feet and legs for strength in balance and readiness for jumps.

**Exercises**

- Begin with a simple ballet partnering exercise focused on one partner assisting the balance of their partner. The supportive partner places their hands at the supported partner's waist to help find verticality and ease of balance in sous-sous relevé, sur le coup de pied, passé, and low attitude devant.
- Exercise 14, Promenade, requires students to practice various promenades and transitions between positions by changing the supportive grip or even shifting the weight transfer and leg positions of the supported partner. A simple assisted pirouette builds on the balance exercise with which students began.
- Exercise 15, Traditional Lifts, begins with stationary assisted jumps and then moves to assisted traveling jumps like grand jeté and pas de chat lifts.

**Final Exploration: Partnered Ballet Phrase**

Link the skills explored in this class with smooth transitions to create a phrase that incorporates assisted balance, promenades, and stationary and traveling lifts.

# Practical Skills and Frameworks for Teaching Dance Partnering: Part I

This section presents the nuts and bolts of creating a foundation for beginning dance partnering instruction. Exercises 1 to 6 underscore and frame solid approaches for the first few weeks of partnering classes. These approaches range from explorations that develop tactile sensitivity and physical listening to guided improvisations that introduce fundamental partnering concepts like weight sharing and counterbalance. These fundamental skills create the foundation on which students build toward an even more dynamic partnering experience in the weeks to come, as detailed in the following chapters. An overview of the exercises follows:

- Exercise 1, Grasp and Clasp, introduces the variety and nuance of touch and connection through the hands.
- Exercise 2, Body Mapping and Trust Building, expands the use of touch and partner responsibility with little to no weight-bearing. Guided body care, anatomical patterning, and trust-building explorations aim to increase student confidence and comfort with being vulnerable.
- Exercise 3, Active and Passive, introduces weight-bearing explorations organized at a low level and with low risk so students experience supporting a partner's weight more safely and fully.
- Exercise 4, Weight Sharing, introduces students to bearing weight in a more mutual framework and serves as the basis for contact improvisation, contemporary partnering, and more advanced exercises introduced in chapters 3 and 4.
- Exercise 5, Counterbalance, teaches skills that open possibilities for smooth and nuanced transitions and serve as the foundation for skills used in social dance and both ballet and contemporary partnering.
- Exercise 6, Shelves and Ledges, concludes this section by introducing students to the mechanics of providing stable surfaces of support to take a partner's full or partial weight and building toward movement of the partner through space when used in later exercises.

EXERCISE 1
## GRASP AND CLASP

### Background

Because the palms contain many nerve receptors, simple connections have the potential to foster nuanced sensitivity and physical listening—serving as a bridge for receptive connections between partners. The hands are an important part of daily human communication. Positive, open interaction is communicated through a wave hello, an extended helping hand, or a thumbs-up signal for a job well done; negative hand expressions range from insensitive, rude gestures to aggression wielded in violence. Thus, the politics of touch that come with the territory of hand-based connection and communication cannot be ignored. In dance partnering, it is vital to creating a safe and trusting environment in a classroom and guide students through exercises that develop sensitivity, nuance, and receptivity in the use of their hands. Connections through the hands are particularly significant because they are common in ballet partnering, modern partnering, ballroom, and social dance.

### Purpose

Exercises exploring the functionality and sensitivity of hand-to-hand touch (grasp, clasp, and grip) are key to creating the base for confidence and reliable connections in more advanced, risky, and momentum-based partnering in the future. As students understand and develop this sensitivity, they eventually sense a partner's weight, center of balance, direction of motion, and base of support—all through hand connection if they are energetically connecting their limbs to their body center.

### In Practice: Grasp and Clasp

Objective: To understand the sensitivity and connection arising from hand-to-hand contact and wrist-to-wrist contact, and to explore the lower forearm and hand as a bridge for connection.

#### TIPS OF THE FINGER

Partners A and B connect fingertip to fingertip. Identify the softness of this degree of connection. Partner A leads partner B through space through the fingertip bridge. What is the smallest degree of touch possible before contact is lost?

#### HANDSHAKE

Partner A offers their hand as if to shake partner B's hand. Notice the degrees of rigidity, tension, or softness within the grasp. Explore the degrees of a handshake and notice the placement of the body during the handshake.

#### LINKING

Partner B offers an open hand to partner A. Each person's palm opens to the forearm of their partner. Find the link between forearm to forearm. How can students use this link to push and pull each other through space?

### Modifications and Problem-Solving

If a student cannot connect with the hand or wrist, please see the mirroring exercise, Generative Prompts and Partnered Compositional Methods, outlined in chapter 4. Allowing a touch-averse student to mirror or echo their partner can foster their connection while avoiding touch entirely. Reservations about and aversion to touch present a challenge to authentic explorations of hand-to-hand contact. Understanding of a student's severe challenges with touch can be achieved through clear communication and dialogue in groups and individually and through review of the syllabus and other instructional materials at the beginning of a course or workshop series. Chapter 5 further describes inclusive pedagogy and provides tips for creating an open, safe environment.

> *continued*

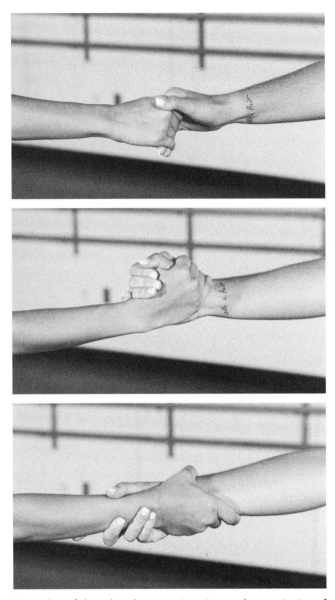

Examples of three hand connections (top to bottom): tips of the finger, handshake, and linking.

## Expanding and Advanced Skills

### SHIFTING SURFACES

For advanced dancers, prompt the class to combine and explore the fingertip, handshake, and linking connections with their partner. Develop a flux and flow between these different ways to connect. By exploring connections through the hands in improvisation, students can begin to access transitions and increase flow by shifting the surfaces of their hands and points of contact with their partner.

## EXERCISE 2
## TRUST BUILDING AND BODY MAPPING

### Background

Early in any training, it is generally best to allow students learning a new technique, trade, or skill to become more familiar and comfortable with the equipment, material, or process used. In partnering, this familiarization period can take many forms but generally involves students becoming more confident in their ability as a reliable partner who can support weight, respond, and adapt so their partner feels secure. Conversely, guided low-risk, low-weight-bearing explorations that familiarize partnering students with the reality and responsibility of engaging with another person go a long way in boosting their confidence and engagement. Ease students in rather than overwhelm them with exercises and explorations that ask too much, too soon.

Just as educators use anatomical visual references or life-sized model skeletons to assist students in deeper understanding of the body (the instrument of dancing), this learning can be fostered through exploration of the structure, mechanics, and motion potential learned from direct interaction with peers' bodies. Guided body work, such as basic massage, traction, and passive mobilization, has the benefits of (1) warming up or soothing sore bodies; (2) increasing student ease, comfort, and sensitivity by engaging other bodies; and (3) serving as a living, life-sized model and body map to further student understanding of anatomy, physiology, and kinesiology.

### Purpose

Simply put, dedicated exercises aimed to foster and develop trust (between partners, with the instructor, and within the broad community of students) form the foundation of confidence, reliability, and sensitivity that go a long way when attempting more complex and risky partnering skills. Body mapping helps students gain broad understanding of body structure and function, which in turn can inform the integration and articulation of their own body when dancing alone and with partners. Mapping has the added benefit of teaching students practical skills for self-care and body maintenance and the ability to care for others in a field where physical therapy, massage, and body care are sometimes limited and often prohibitively expensive.

### In Practice: Trust Building and Body Mapping

Objective: To build a sense of one's body in space, to foster a sense of other bodies within the space, to read the room, to condition the neuromuscular connection by way of touch, and to become skilled at receiving touch.

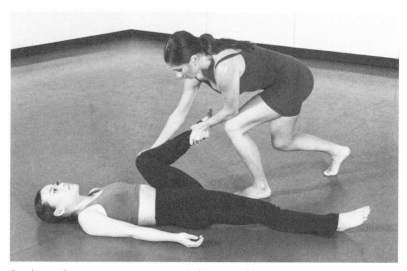

Students demonstrate passive mobilization of the leg in the body mapping exercise.

> continued

## BODY MAPPING

A sense of the body in space can often be curated visually. Lying on the ground, partner A closes their eyes and gets a sense of their own body through partnered massage and touch. Partner B claps their hands together above partner A's head. Partner A tunes into their senses immediately. Partner B rubs their hands together to produce heat. Once partner B's hands are warm, they begin with the right side of partner A's shoulder and follow the length of the arm, massaging or pressing while communicating with partner A regarding the degree of touch. Mapping can continue (at the discretion of the instructor and students) to distal parts of the body, such as the opposite arm, legs, fingers, and toes, and toward the trunk.

## ▶ BODY MAPPING WITH PASSIVE MOBILIZATION

Two students demonstrate a basic partnered somatic exercise.

### TRUSTING: GUIDED EXPLORATION WITHOUT SIGHT

Partner A guides partner B with eyes closed (or blindfolded), helping them to sit, stand, and navigate hallways and studio spaces. Partner A trusts partner B with their body in space. Although this task is simple, the guiding partner must take great care with the partner they are leading. For the guided partner, this is a low-impact option to build trust and bond students.

### Modifications and Problem-Solving

While the relative simplicity of this early exercise may not warrant significant modifications, discomfort with touch or the potential intimacy of body mapping can be avoided by guiding students to map their own bodies and consider the same principles as they would with a partner. Although more can be gained from exploration with a partner, the anatomical aspects that an instructor may want to introduce can be explored individually.

Similarly, if the vulnerability of exploring with eyes closed is too uncomfortable for some students, the same exercise can be offered with eyes open. Although the disorientation of closed eyes builds greater trust, one student can still lead and guide the other; this introduces physical listening if the student can follow the partner guiding them and not override with their own decision making.

### Expanding and Advanced Skills

Partners A and B challenge the degree of trust and ability to sense one another in space. With their eyes closed, partners A and B forge a connection in space through information received through touch. While exploring in this mode, both partners must remain sensitive to and malleable with one another and continue to sense external obstacles and peers while exploring.

EXERCISE 3
## ACTIVE AND PASSIVE

### Background

The floor-bound exercise at the root of this concept is drawn from creative explorations experienced in rehearsals with Shen Wei in the development of his piece *Re-II* (Wei 2007). This exploration allows for the full release of the supported partner's weight (passive), which the supportive partner (active) mobilizes through space. The active and passive exercise relates to some foundational contact improvisation exercises and principles, and it uses low-risk weight-bearing and support through skills such as shelving and draping (exercises 6 and 7). Practicing these dynamics also allows the supportive partner to develop a greater sense of push and pull and integrated use of all limbs for leverage in low-level movement. More complex expressions of the active and passive dynamic (discussed in later chapters) are present in exercise 16, Initiation and Suggestion, and exercise 17, Rolling Points, among others. What serves functionally as an opportunity to exchange taking responsibility for each other's weight also allows students to develop deeper physical listening skills and explore more sensitive, weighted connections to their partners.

Partners in a perpendicular orientation to demonstrate a useful starting position for the active and passive exercise.

Partners in a slightly higher shape to demonsrate the active partner supporting the passive partner's weight at a low to medium level.

> *continued*

**ACTIVE AND PASSIVE >** *continued*

## Purpose

Active and passive exercises serve as excellent frameworks for developing give and take, fully yielding and receiving weight with a partner, and honing nuanced transitions between the active and passive roles. As dancers understand this flux between two seemingly opposite states, they can begin to inhabit both active and passive sensibilities almost simultaneously. These skill sets foster an elastic, responsive quality in a partner's dancing that is particularly useful in improvised partnering in which action, response, and attentive listening are vital to the ease of flow and interaction. Both taking initiative when opportunities arise and following a partner's impulses and initiations make for excellent partnership and incredibly articulate and mature dancing. When a dancer learns to keep this heightened awareness and presence even in familiar, choreographed material, magic is possible on stage.

## Foundational Exercises

### GUIDED IMPROVISATION

Guide dancers through a solo exploration of push and pull while maintaining a floor-bound, low level. Draw attention to the fold and crease of the hips, knees, ankles, elbows, wrists, and the highly mobile shoulder joints to shift their weight, driven by tactile hands and feet. Encourage students to find other surfaces of support in low- to mid-level improvisation. Find the broad surface of the lats, outer thighs, shins, and sides of the shoulder and upper arm to locate other potential bases of support and allow for more unique movement potential.

### WORKSHOPPING

It can be useful to reduce a concept into smaller, lower-stakes versions for exploration before attempting the full expression, particularly with dancers new to partnering training. For a precursor to active and passive exploration, guide dancers through workshopping of the concept with just the weight of the arm. Standing together, partner A (supportive or active) will take the weight of partner B's arm (supported or passive); once the weight is fully released, partner A can begin to mobilize and guide partner B in maintaining full support of the arm. In this exploration, partner B must work to release the weight of their arm, keep a soft malleable shoulder, and try to listen to the physical guidance of their partner while also maintaining a supple yet self-supported posture overall. To deepen the experience, students support a partner's released head weight. Taking care to support the head and neck, the supported partner can fall and spill through the space with head weight as the motivator. Students often respond well to this exploration but it can be more intense, particularly when the supportive partner has to support the other dancer's head with a hand in contact with their partner's face. When that discomfort is overcome, the feeling of dancing while releasing head weight into supportive hands is incredible. A sensation of floating and suspension arises that is almost impossible to feel while dancing alone but might have the secondary benefit of helping dancers understand the benefit of using the weight of the head while dancing in general.

## In Practice: Active and Passive

Objective: To listen while pouring weight, exchanging the effect of softening to release, and engaging to mobilize.

### YIELDING AND BREATHING: FROM THE GROUND UP

Begin with partner A taking a prone position on the floor. They might lie on their back, front, or side. Partner B lies perpendicularly on top of partner A. Before partners move or mobilize, allow time for them to breathe and feel the sensations of giving and receiving weight, respectively. The diaphragmatic breathing action of both partners might even line up with one partner inhaling while the other is exhaling. An advanced, more intimate version of this weight-sensing practice can be offered (perhaps as an option or reserved for university or professional levels). One partner lies face up on the ground in an anatomical position, with their arms at low diagonals and palms facing up. Their partner stacks entirely on top of them, face down. This can be intensely intimate and physically challenging but has incredible somatic benefits when maintained for at least 10 to 15 minutes, or more.

### ACTIVE AND PASSIVE MOTIVATION THROUGH SPACE

Moving on from yielding and breathing, partner B relaxes and then drapes over and releases into their partner, distributing their weight broadly like a blanket. Once this full release of weight is felt, partner A uses the push and pull of their hands and feet and folding of their joints to guide and mobilize themselves and their draping partner through space. Have students practice seamlessly switching roles and developing sensitive transitions between them. It is important for this exploration to begin and maintain a slow, careful pace; when weight is shifted too quickly, momentum can cause a disconnect or spillover action in the supported partner. As quickly becomes obvious, a key factor in this exploration is learning to sense the transition between active and passive roles. This exchange continues for the entire exercise. Students must explore when they need to yield and release and when to activate and support their partner during a transition between roles. Video demonstrations of this active and passive exercise highlight this transitional awareness.

### ▶ ACTIVE AND PASSIVE

Early exploration of active and passive concept through improvisation.

### Modifications and Problem-Solving

Common challenges in this exploration are linked to students not truly releasing weight to allow their partner to sense, support, and mobilize them. The release of weight provides a tactile, physical feedback source that a supportive partner can then push into to move their partner's weight center. Another common issue arises when partners end up too parallel, leading to an effect akin to two hotdogs rolling side by side on a gas station warmer. To avoid or adjust out of this situation, dancers should be instructed to fold and direct their weight up and over their partner perpendicularly before they begin to release their weight in the passive role. Sometimes, dancers fold and roll in the same relationship to one another, effectively repeating the same transition. When this occurs, instruct active partner students to check the folding in of limbs underneath their body to lift, rotate, and reposition their passive partner. Attending to changing the surfaces of connection can also be helpful; shift between back-to-back, front-to-back, side-to-back, and side-to-front relationships, and other movements and transitions will emerge.

### Expanding and Advanced Skills

In an advanced, more intimate version of the yielding and breathing weight-sensing practice, one partner lies face up on the ground in an anatomical position, with their arms at low diagonals and palms facing up. Their partner stacks entirely on top of them, face down. This exercise can be intensely intimate and physically challenging and can be offered as an advanced option or reserved for university or professional levels. For the right group of students or dancers in a creative process, it can foster deeper bonds, give a more complete sense of truly releasing one's weight, and have incredible somatic benefits when maintained for 15 to 20 minutes. Like the newly popular weighted blankets or thunder jackets for animals, this practice can be wonderfully calming and reduce anxiety.

## WEIGHT SHARING

### Background

Weight within a partnering context can be linked to its study in a technique class of many genres. Weight sharing is not unique to partner work. For example, the vertical sense of shared weight into the floor within a ballet class can be a useful tool and sensation to acknowledge in partnering settings. Modern dance floor routines require dancers to take weight into parts of the body. By asking students to acknowledge their own connection between weight and their center of gravity, they can then be ready for and acknowledge another person's gravity and weight distribution.

### Purpose

Exercises that explore the functionality of weight sharing are key to creating a genuine connection for partnered explorations. Just like weight into the floor can propel dancers through space, weight in partner work can build reliable connections to then react and forge a greater range of choreographic and technical choice. As students further understand weight sharing with another person, they eventually sense the freedom that comes from nontraditional modes of support.

### Foundational Exercise

WORKSHOPPING: THE WALL

Dancers use a wall to experience weight on the vertical. First, they explore weight through the hands, similar to a vertical push-up. Then they pour their weight into the wall in a vertical alignment. How does it feel different from giving weight on the horizontal? Zoning into the trunk of the dancer, how is weight sharing different with variations in pelvic alignment (tucked, neutral, or tilted pelvis)?

### In Practice: Weight Sharing

Objective: To give weight and receive weight using a shared surface area.

PICK AND WEIGH

Instruct students to pick three areas of the body and identify how they can connect and serve as areas of contact. Have students connect their selected body zones to their partner's point or points of contact, plié, soften their knees, and then pour their weight into the point of contact while moving their legs and feet (base of support) gradually farther away from one another, which will increase the degree of weight shared. The direc-

Like the yoga ball exercise, practicing weight sharing first with a wall allows students to understand their alignment before attempting it with a partner.

tion of weight falling is toward (and through) their partner, with a wide base of support away from the other and the shared plumb line between partners running directly below the primary point of contact. Each partner's plumb line runs diagonally up from their feet to the top of their head, angling in toward the shared plumb line. Figure 2.1 presents a visual diagram of these alignment dynamics. See the video resources on weight-sharing exercises for explanations of how dynamics apply in more complex variations.

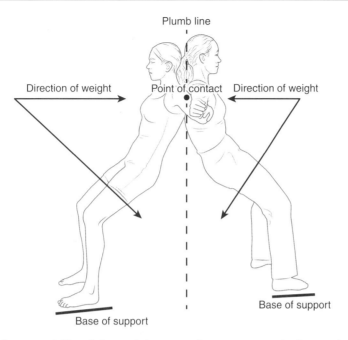

**FIGURE 2.1**   A linear, visual breakdown of alignment dynamics in weight sharing depicting the structural makeup of a partnered weight-sharing movement.

Partners explore basic weight-sharing positions. What variations can you find?

> continued

### Modifications and Problem-Solving

In weight sharing, communication is key for authentic giving and receiving of weight. From an outsider's perspective, students may appear to have each other's weight or perhaps one partner has more weight than their fellow dancer. Therefore, maintaining a verbal exchange between partners can be helpful in weight sharing. Encourage empathic thinking and questioning. Ask students to consider this question: How would this be different for my partner if I gave them more or less weight?

The instructor may aid in the nuanced exploration of weight sharing by observing and highlighting obvious challenges. In the receiving and giving of weight, students may tuck or release their lower back to give weight. A non-reinforced pelvic floor distributes weight across the body differently than contact with a dancer through a stable, connected relationship between the trunk and lower body. Weight sharing in advanced explorations can benefit from a reminder that touch and contact have varied degrees of effort, momentum, and release. By visiting exercise 1, Grasp and Clasp, and other examples, reinforcement of self-realized power and sensitivity can heighten and allow for authentic weight sharing.

### Expanding and Advanced Skills

Once students are comfortable with falling into one another and stabilizing shared weight, more advanced variations can be explored. When balance and ease is found in a given weight-sharing action, partnerships slowly move their bases of support farther away. This increases the degree of weight being shared, challenges core strength to maintain overall shape, and moves toward lowering and rising into and out of the floor via weight sharing. Advanced variations include exploring the rise from and fall to the floor while maintaining weight sharing; locomoting across the room in a weight share, moving the feet in a shared direction; and revolving around the center plumb line, moving the feet around clockwise or counterclockwise. An exploration of weight share in which weight becomes less equal between partners involves one partner driving into the point of contact with more weight and pressure and moving the shape toward their partner's feet, similar to a linebacker in American football driving into their counterpart on the opposing team. With less intensity and increased sensitivity, partners can maintain the weight share even with unequal degrees of weight between them.

### ▶ WEIGHT SHARING

Early exploration of weight sharing, shifting connections with smooth transitions, and rotation.

EXERCISE 5
## COUNTERBALANCE

### Background

The vertically oriented exploration at the root of this exercise derives from the negotiation of gravity with a partnered through line. Organized tension and pull are required within a counterbalance as partners explore center of gravity with an off-center relationship. This exploration allows for cultivation of full trust. Visually, audiences are enthralled by counterbalance and its embodiment of risk. Counterbalance, as the name suggests, is predicated on the oppositional force of released weight. Through this opposition, dancers can create a point of balance. Counterbalances often are visually exciting and can transition into other partnered explorations, such as promenades and changes in level. By serving functionally as an opportunity to oppose the space, counterbalance allows students to develop a deeper physical understanding of tension, connection, and weight distribution.

### Purpose

Exercises exploring the functionality of counterbalance are essential to creating a dynamic partnership. Not all partnering is proximal. Just as dancers like to travel through space, partner work can be kinetically explosive, risky, and physical. As students begin to understand what counterbalance is with another person, they can eventually sense the freedom that comes from being off-center through a shared link with a partner.

### Foundational Exercise

WORKSHOPPING: HANGING

Here, students practice on their own. First, they go to a barre on the wall or stand on opposite sides of a freestanding barre. They then take a firm hold with their feet close to the wall or barre, soften their knees, and hang away, just as a ballet dancer stretches their back by hanging away from the barre. Students then release one hand, hang away sideways, and lengthen and soften their legs. Make sure that the pelvis is generally in line with the body and not directing the weight back over their base of support. This foundational exercise offers the perfect opportunity to check in with students on pelvic alignment before they work with partners.

### In Practice: Counterbalance

Objective: To discover balance through connection with another person by hanging weight centers away from a shared point of contact.

HANGING OUT

Start by having students use a firm wrist-lock grasp (as in exercise 1, Grasp and Clasp) and face their partner. They stand closely with elbows bent, soften their knees into a demi plié, and lean back away from one another, gradually extending their arms. They explore keeping the body long and hanging away with extended arms, and then they should try sinking down with bent knees (like sitting in a chair) and rounding their back. Offer a variation that uses one hand in a cross-body handshake grasp. Students keep their shoulders facing one another by engaging the biceps of the working arm. They allow the shoulder to open and hang sideways relative to their partner. Their weight falls horizontally away from their partner, with the base of support close together, and the shared plumb line between partners runs directly below the primary point of contact. Opposite of weight sharing, each partner's individual plumb line runs diagonally up from their feet to the top of their head but angles away from the shared plumb line. Figure 2.2 presents a visual diagram of these alignment dynamics. See the video resources on counterbalance exercises for explanations of how dynamics still apply in more complex variations.

▶ COUNTERBALANCE

Early exploration of counterbalance, with variations demonstrated by two different pairs of students.

> continued

**COUNTERBALANCE** > *continued*

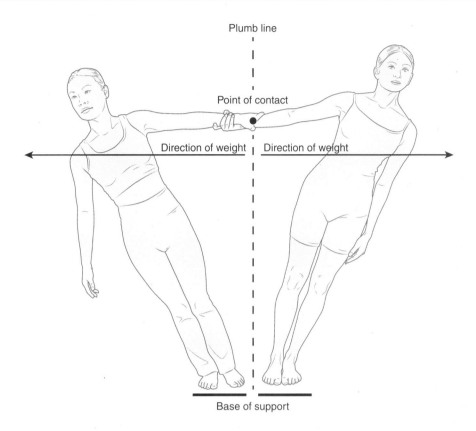

**FIGURE 2.2**  A linear, visual breakdown of alignment dynamics in counterbalance.

Students present a balanced symmetrical expression of counterbalance.

## Modifications and Problem-Solving

Common challenges in this exploration most often result from students not reinforcing the authentic link between them. The pull of weight provides a sense of physical feedback that a supportive partner can then negotiate. Sometimes partners end up too close to one another, leading to an effect like a handshake. To avoid or adjust out of this situation, instruct students to recognize the distance required for a true counterbalance. Dancers sometimes find they are in a counterbalance that is not balanced. This allocation of pull from one partner to another is the exciting balance associated with counterbalance. By softening the elbow and engaging the biceps, slight adjustments can be made to the degree of weight hanging away. If a student feels that their weight is out of balance with their partner's weight, they can bend their arm and pull themselves toward their plumb line to lessen their weight or extend their arm to add weight.

## Expanding and Advanced Skills

As with weight sharing, more advanced variations can be explored once pairs have learned the basics of counterbalance. Next, have students explore asymmetrical connections and positions and connect with body parts other than the hands. For example, they can hook elbows, put one hand to the shoulder or waist of a partner with free hands, or flex the foot and hook behind their partner's calf or back of the knee. Other advanced variations include rising from and falling to the floor while maintaining counterbalance; locomoting across the room in a counterbalance hanging away from the point of contact, moving the feet in a shared direction; and revolving around the center plumb line, moving the feet around clockwise or counterclockwise. Explore morphing the connections and orientations between partners, slowly shifting and changing while continuously maintaining the counterbalance.

Students present a balanced, asymmetrical expression of counterbalance with unique connection.

## EXERCISE 6
## SHELVES AND LEDGES

### Background

A central technique for the practice of contact improvisation is for one dancer to offer flat, broad, and stable body surfaces to support their partner's weight. Depending on the orientation between partners, connection points, and stance, posture, or architecture of the supportive partner, these surfaces might support the full or partial weight of the supported partner (Novack 1990).

In contact improvisation and related contemporary partnering forms, these stable, supportive surfaces are known as *shelves* or *ledges*. Although they are most prevalent in these forms, they are applied in classical ballet partnering as well. One common example is the glorious wrapped-fish lift, in which the supportive partner takes a strong sideways lunge to support the hips of the supported ballet dancer with their legs wrapped back around their partner to sustain leverage for an upright presentational posture.

Even ballet partnering uses elements related to shelving from contact improvisation. The thigh of the supportive partner provides a shelf for the hips of the supported partner.

Erik Isakson/Corbis/Getty Images

### Purpose

Shelves are most commonly used to support a partner beyond the use of hands alone. Providing alternate surfaces of the body allows for more complex and unique connections and movement in and out of support to create seamless transitions and flow. With experience and practice, these shelves can be mobilized to execute supported lifts that travel in space.

### Foundational Exercises

#### GUIDED IMPROVISATION

With students dancing alone at first, lead them through a floor-bound improvisational exploration focused on body architecture and structure. Draw attention to their use of hands, feet, knees, and elbows to support their own weight and architectural body postures that will become stable surfaces (shelves) for their partner.

### Workshopping

Before open exploration of this concept, the instructor can demonstrate or use two student volunteers to illustrate and explain that with any posture a supportive partner takes, there are green zones (the strongest points in any structure) and red zones (the weakest points). A clear first example might be to have the supportive partner take a table-top position on their hands and knees. The supported partner can then test the strength of various zones on the broad surface of their partner's back from shoulders to pelvis. In doing so, they recognize that the green zones are across the shoulders and pelvis where the hands and knees are the bases of support respective to the shoulders and hips. A red zone is the mid-back or waist area, farthest from a base of support. This is not to say that a strong, experienced partner cannot provide adequate shelf support in this area. However, for safety and clarity in a beginner-level class, identifying these zones and fostering this consideration of the supportive partner can help avoid injury and discomfort in early explorations of shelves and ledges.

## ▶ SHELVES AND LEDGES

Partners alternate between supported and supportive roles, explore how to transition between shapes on a supportive shelf, and alternate to create a shelf for their partner.

### In Practice: Shelves and Ledges

Objective: To understand the connection arising from points of contact other than hand-to-hand contact and practicing the tone of contact.

### STACKING

Consider the floor to be the broadest shelf, and encourage students to find ways to lie down. Partners A and B connect from the floor and build from the floor up, similar to the game Jenga. Partner A lies on their back, and partner B lies directly on top perpendicularly. Then partner B lies on their right side. Partner A lies on their right side, stacking on the shelf of partner B. The partners communicate with each other and notice the sensation of receiving and offering weight.

### TABLE TOP

Partner A stacks their shoulders over their hands, with their elbows lengthened but not locked. Their knees are directly under their hips. Partner B finds four points of contact over partner A: left wrist to partner B's left shoulder, right wrist to partner B's shoulder, left knee to left hip or glute, and right knee to right hip or glute. Consider how each partner can give weight to the table.

Table-top shelving: Practicing shelving in low-level support allows students to ease into this exploration of full weight-bearing.

> *continued*

### STANDING

Partner B stands with their knees with a wide base (second position rotated, in parallel lunge, wide parallel fourth position). Partner A explores giving weight to the lower body of partner B. Avoid grasps and clasps. Examples include sitting on partner B, with the tailbone to the most stable point.

## Modifications and Problem-Solving

Students may be apprehensive about contact that requires connecting larger body surface areas to their partner. Framing this progression as a continuation of floor work and floor connectivity can stimulate shared weight. Postural challenges often arise when students attempt to provide surfaces or ledges that are not aligned near or above a base of support, resulting in a weaker foundation for connection. A collapse of the lower back indicates a disengaged core.

Standing and shelving: Practicing shelving at mid-level support allows students to find more dynamic explorations of shelving.

## Expanding and Advanced Skills

### ENGINEERING SUPPORT

Partners A and B explore shelves and ledges through an improvisation including stacking, table top, and standing. Practice transitions between shelves on different levels without touching the ground. Explore the nuance of gradually giving weight to take support, emphasizing transitions, ease, and efficiency. Introduce riskier ledges like the shoulders while standing upright. Encourage an interplay between the supportive partner guiding the other toward additional ledges and the supported partner taking an active role in climbing and finding new supportive surfaces.

Taking shelving to higher levels can add excitement and dynamic interaction between partners but shares the same principles as low-level, table-top shelf support.

## SUMMARY

This chapter introduced the book's practical offerings in support of curriculum planning and individual class design to prepare readers for custom combinations and utilization of the information to come. Part I of the Practical Skills and Frameworks for Teaching Dance Partnering series started with low-risk, low-weight-bearing exercises to set the stage for more challenging and complex exercises in the following chapters.

Chapter 3, Weight: Digging Deeper, frames techniques and exercises that prepare the body and build strength and stability over time. With guidance on effective cross-training, injury prevention, breath work, and sequenced warm-ups, chapter 3 offers insights that are important to consider for adequate preparation for the unique demands of dance partnering training. Part II of Practical Skills and Frameworks for Teaching Dance Partnering outlines another grouping of exercises that build on the skills learned in chapter 2.

## DISCUSSION QUESTIONS

1. What are your dance values? When you plan a course, what skills, aesthetics, or dynamics do you seek to cultivate in your students?

2. Think of your educational setting. What are the primary goals of the curricular thrust?

3. What goals have your students set for themselves? How might curricular planning decisions center on student needs and goals?

4. When preparing for a single master class or guest artist engagement, what are three takeaways that you hope students will leave with?

For additional information, see the ancillary materials and resources linked to this chapter in HK*Propel.*

Brandon Whited and Shelby Caputo in
*Petit Pas.* Santa Barbara Dance Theater.
Choreography by Brandon Whited.

# WEIGHT: Digging Deeper

## OVERVIEW

Preparing students to succeed within the physical demands of partnering is a thrilling and challenging task. As new physical connections and possibilities emerge in the partnering classroom, conditioning practices and cross-training can prepare dancers for new ways to explore space and sense of weight. Where does the foundation for partnering training begin on a physical level? How can a warm-up or series of exercises prepare students for the physical demands associated with partnering? This chapter considers the body as a complex instrument and discusses safe techniques and foundational biomechanics, frameworks for cross-training and preparatory strengthening for partnering, promotion of self-care and dancer wellness, and, when appropriate, techniques for partnered somatic body work, mutual care, and maintenance.

### VOCABULARY

360-degree core
center of balance
centripetal force
contralateral
eccentric
homolateral
isometric

isotonic
mobility challenge
pranayama
somatics
synergy
traction

Although partnering can achieve a beautiful harmony of movement, often to such a degree that viewers remain unaware of the mechanical effort involved within the connection, a focused amount of physical effort and concentration is required within partnering practice and training. By exploring the body's kinesthetic potential, dancers have a greater opportunity to create efficient and safe approaches to their partnering practice. This chapter describes safe techniques and foundational biomechanics in dancer partnering and offers dedicated exercises in part II of Practical Skills and Frameworks for Teaching Dance Partnering.

## Safe Techniques and Foundational Biomechanics: The Body as a Source of Knowledge

Teachers can pour their knowledge of anatomy and somatics into the partnering classroom. In fact, partnering practice often lends to discussions that the body, with its intricately woven system of levers and efficient anatomical chains, has a built-in source of knowledge. Within a partnering context, the distribution of weight between two dancers can mean the difference between injury or joyful efficiency of sharing momentum, connection, and weight. Start by reminding students that the energy, focus, and physical awareness they bring to their physical practice affects their partnering abilities. If a partnering practice can greatly increase knowledge of one's own biomechanical structure and support system, teachers and choreographers can readily share that partnerships within the context of class or rehearsal will tax dancers' coordination, strength, endurance, and flexibility. With luck, before the teacher can discuss these benefits, they learn that their students already possess a love for partnering for that reason; however, these exciting moments come with challenges and exertion in the form of shared inertia, momentum, power, and intricacies in timing. Partnering is mesmerizing and can be recognized for the attributes of a connection, a synergy that must come with care and guidance.

Power comes from a source. Energy can be drawn from a supportive, physical foundation or *sense of weight*. In other words, the body's engaged connection and energy originate from a grounded connection to the floor. As explained in chapter 2 in exercise 4, Weight Sharing, efficient use of one's power rooted in this base of support provides access to leverage and thrust. Learning about the capabilities of the lower body is essential within the partnering context because all partnering is subject to gravity. Likewise, care and stimulation of the lower body prepares students for technical play and investigation. It is imperative that teachers share their knowledge of the lower body's potential and biomechanical capabilities and describe how the lower body integrates into the core or weight center. For example, in partnering contexts, the instructor taps into dancer recollection of basic knee-to-ankle traction, examination of weight distribution in a supporting foot (Fitt 1996), and acknowledgment of hip rotation, placement, and range of motion (Fitt 1996). Therefore, warm-ups adequate for a partnering class are suggested, and several explorations and exercises within the following sections can adequately prepare dancers.

Body strength and stability are not the only safety concerns in partnering. In basic partnering, function is more important than fashion. Identifying a space for phrase work or particular explorations is key. Empower students with the notion that by taking a partnering class, they are considering the safety and well-being of their peers. Discuss appropriate rehearsal and class attire. Baggy clothing, jewelry, and accessories can be unsafe and a hindrance for dancers to navigate safely within the class. Footwear is perhaps one of the largest concerns in present-day classrooms, which often call for the use of socks to reduce friction in particular contemporary dance styles. As noted later in the exercise sequences, friction can play a role in task efficiency, depending on the exploration. The use of socks makes a frictionless surface for an exercise like a promenade, whereas dancing barefoot allows dancers to root into the ground and then effectively redirect energy. Bare feet are particularly important in weight sharing, counterbalance exercises, and off-center movements that require grip and purchase for the partner in a supportive role.

To maintain safety, instruct students to (1) avoid wearing jewelry, (2) secure their hair (particularly longer hair), and (3) maintain proper hand and body hygiene. Dangling jewelry and three-dimensional rings can catch, cut, scratch, or injure a partner and should be avoided. Long hair becomes a whip when practicing partnering skills with rapid turns or rotations and can easily pull or snag. Dancers with longer hair should secure it in a ponytail or bun. Personal hygiene is a sensitive subject, but students are less likely to feel targeted if it is addressed early and in a group setting. Request that students keep their fingernails and toenails relatively short and smooth to avoid cutting, gouging, or scratching a partner. Proper personal hygiene and oral hygiene are important for comfort and ease between partners but also reduce germ spread. Encourage thorough handwashing, and avoiding touching one's face, mouth, and eyes while working, both before and after a partnering class. Proper laundering of rehearsal clothes, costumes, and undergarments is also important.

## Cross-Training and Preparatory Strengthening

Preparing students for partnering means that their body must be ready to receive external force while negotiating internal cues and sensations. Dancers must learn about the relationship between their distal points and their sense of core. Core work for partnering goes beyond the study of the abdominal muscles. The core can be thought of as a 360-degree connection that includes the abdominal and back muscles. Often, dancers think of front body core engagement or traditional sit-ups as the sole source of core exploration. Stress to students that the core involves the side, back, and front. In partnering, the link between the periphery and core contributes to the fun that dancers can experience when they are aware of their strength, range of motion, and power. In *Harnessing the Wind*, Jan Erkert reminds teachers that conditioning means "facilitating time and energy for the big four: strength, flexibility, muscular endurance, and cardiovascular endurance" (Erkert 2003, 54).

Preparatory strengthening can be broken down into exercises that (1) stabilize and (2) emphasize mobility. This awareness is geared toward asking questions (e.g., What parts of the body are moving? Which part of the body is stable or immobile?) and developing greater knowledge of one's own dancing instrument—the body.

Exercises focused on isometric muscle contraction help build stability and strength while maintaining mobility and suppleness in a dancer's movement. Think of it as developing tensile strength in the body, or muscle tone over bulk. Isometric muscle contraction describes muscular action or initiation in which muscle length remains the same (table 3.1). The muscle is engaged without movement of the limbs or structures connected to it. In this way, isometric action in the muscles is a central building block toward many aspects of the strength required for dance partnering.

Spinal mobility and stability are essential explorations for partnering. In a supportive partnering role, this translates to having control over what might be moving or still. By exploring isometric connections, dancers can draw on their understanding of what they can connect to support their partner. Conversely, if a lift or partnered connection is free and unbound, the dancer's ability to respond and release the body is key. Teachers can return to the floor at any point and remind students that ebb and flow, toning and releasing, are

**TABLE 3.1**   Common Isometric Positions

| Position | Example |
| --- | --- |
| Double-leg forearm plank | Plank with both legs connected to the floor |
| Single-leg forearm plank | Plank with one leg lifted off the floor |
| Double-leg elbow plank | Low plank with both legs connected to the floor |
| Single-leg elbow plank | Low plank with one leg lifted off the floor |
| Double-leg side plank | Side plank with both legs connected to the floor |
| Single-leg side plank | Side plank with one leg lifted off the floor |

| Position | Example |
|---|---|
| Double-leg short plank | Plank with the knees stacked under the hips, hovering |
| Single-leg short plank | Plank with the knees stacked under the hips, hovering with the leg lifted off the floor |
| Double-leg glute bridge | Bridge with both legs connected to the floor |
| Single-leg glute bridge | Bridge with one leg lifted off the floor |

essential actions within connection. By zoning into the space between the low ribs and hip tips and examining the possibilities of the axial skeleton, teachers can curate isometric core work that challenges mobility. In these training exercises, positions that activate and engage the core are made more challenging by mobilizing another body part. That additional movement increases the challenges (and benefits) of a particular action (table 3.2).

## ▶ TABLE 3.2

Exercises described in table 3.2 are also available on video.

Incorporate isometric positions with asymmetrical variations. Lifting the limbs in a contralateral fashion while in a plank position (e.g., the left hand forward with the right leg off the ground) will prepare students for the compound weight sharing and balance required in partnered explorations. Core engagement with abdominal flexion allows students to activate their frontline. Activation of anterior core muscles in partnering, like in contemporary or modern dance, allows dancers to change levels, move swiftly, and

**TABLE 3.2**   Isometric Positions With Mobility Challenges

| Position | Description |
|---|---|
| High plank oblique dips | While in the plank dip, isolate the upper body and mobilize the hips side to side |
| High plank windshield wipers | While in plank, release the hips side to side |
| High plank shin-ups | While in plank, tap the shin bone to the floor |
| Lawn mowers from side plank | While in side plank, reach the free arm in a pulling motion |
| Chest or wide arm push-ups | With the elbows out at 90 degrees, descend through the bending of the arms |
| Triceps push-ups | With elbows hugging the sides of the body, descend through the bending of the arms |
| Scapula push-ups | With arms in plank, release the mid-upper body, allowing the chest to drop between the shoulders and then return to neutral |

| Position | Description |
|---|---|
| Bear crawl  | Crawl by bearing weight on the hands and toes rather than the knees (this is an excellent exercise in core control and focused breathing) |

strengthen their movement. By combining core engagement with isometrics, dancers can get a sense of their three-dimensional structure and increase awareness of their core.

Attention to cross-training works best when the teacher verbally connects the exercise to how it translates to the peak context of class. Therefore, conditioning should make its way to some level of standing work. Encourage translation of the concepts examined for the core to full-body awareness, incorporating the lower body. Empowering the largest muscle group provides not only an opportunity to strengthen it but also space for cardiovascular endurance. If the teacher draws inspiration from classical training, they may gear the first half of class toward articulation of the lower appendicular region (table 3.3).

**TABLE 3.3**  Lower Body–Focused Challenges

| Challenge | Description |
|---|---|
| One-legged hops  | Jump from a position, forward to back and then side to side on one leg |
| Two-legged hops | Jump from a position, forward to back and then side to side on two legs |

**TABLE 3.3** > *continued*

| Challenge | Description |
|---|---|
| Burpees (with or without push-ups) | Jump straight up, squat down, and push back to plank (push-up optional at the bottom) |
| Squat jumps | With hips back and weight in the heels, jump straight up and land in a squat |
| Mountain climbers | In high plank, drive the knee toward the chest in a running motion |
| Double lunges | While standing, bend both legs in a parallel lunged position with one leg forward and one leg behind |

| Challenge | Description |
|---|---|
| Wall sits  | Sit against a wall with the back flush to the wall, and bend the knees at a 90-degree angle with the heels directly underneath |
| Parallel skaters or glissades | Jump side to side, with emphasis on the accent pulling inward |

▶ TABLE 3.3

Exercises described in table 3.3 are also available on video.

Ask students to consider questions like these: What bodily information is necessary for the peak phrase or lift that day or that rehearsal? What muscles and physical coordination are needed? The answers to these questions illustrate the link between exercise and exploration. Also ask students to consider the following: What are the five ways your spine can move? What muscles are activating at the beginning of the lift? Taking weight and understanding physical capabilities translated from partner to partner both call for effective and thoughtful conditioning.

Figures 3.1 to 3.3 provide three COVID-19–inspired workouts to keep people moving at home. By working with weight, force, and gravity in the workout portions of class, students mimic motions and pathways that will connect them to their future partners.

| FIGURE 3.1   Lower Body Workout |
|---|

## LEG WORK

### 5 MINUTES

### One-Legged Standing Work (With or Without Weights)

One-legged squat pulses, eight repetitions
One-legged squat side raises (variations: side, back diagonal, behind), eight repetitions
Around the world, eight pulses in each direction
Shiva squat

### 7 TO 10 MINUTES WITH WEIGHTS

Goblet squat
Goblet squat with a twist
Horse pose with pulses (add weights)
Squat jumps (add weight)
Thrusters with single weight
Hops
Rainbow lunges, holding onto two weights
Alternate the Warrior 2 pose for 30 seconds with the Reverse Warrior pose
Glute bridge raises, alternating legs
Wall sit, knee bends with Yoga ball
Wall sit, stationary - one to two minutes

▶ LOWER BODY WORKOUT

The sequence from figure 3.1 is demonstrated, with actions and titles for the sequence described. Variations are demonstrated with and without weights. Shown as single repetitions.

| FIGURE 3.2   360-Degree Core Workout |
|---|

## 15-MINUTE ABDOMINALS

### FRONT AND SIDE CORE

Low plank, knee to elbow
Supine changement
Sit-up in 1 count, down slow
Hip dips
Corkscrew or Russian Twist
Supine elbow to knee
Flutter kicks
Low plank arabesque

### BACK CORE

Dolphin push-ups
Shoulder taps
Swimming
Back-ups

▶ 360-DEGREE CORE WORKOUT

The sequence from figure 3.2 is demonstrated, with actions and titles for the sequence described. Variations are demonstrated for more challenging options. Shown as single repetitions.

**FIGURE 3.3** Upper Body Workout

**15-MINUTE ARMS**

<u>PILATES PUSH-UPS (TRICEPS PULSES)</u>

Down four pulses and up four pulses, four repetitions

Down one pulse and up three pulses, four repetitions

Down three pulses and up one pulse, four repetitions

Single pulses, eight repetitions

Add pulses

<u>MERMAIDS</u>

One arm–side arm, lying on side

Four presses of four counts each, with one arm in front of the chest

Single presses, eight repetitions

Pulses

<u>SIDE PLANK WITH REACH THROUGH</u>

Elbow and high variations, four repetitions of four

<u>DOWN DOG</u>

Triceps push-ups, four repetitions of four

▶ UPPER BODY WORKOUT

The sequence from figure 3.3 is demonstrated, with actions and titles for the sequence described.

# Promoting Self-Care and Partnered Somatic Bodywork Exercises for Mutual Support

It is important for students of dance partnering technique to prepare the body for strength and stability. In addition to the intensity of the warm-ups offered in the previous section, somatic breath-based exercises can also prepare the body for ease and resiliency and serve as an important component of injury prevention or after-practice body care.

## Embodied Learning: Partnering Practice

As in a contemporary or classical technique setting, the concept of practice is vital to partnering contexts and training environments. A lift, however impressive, is not merely an arrival. The journey and evolution to the connection can be a beautiful promotion of self-awareness and care. Humans are built to move and bend. When dancers realize that they can use these abilities to further another's force, flow, and journey, they become empowered in a new way.

In yoga, one of the most intimidating poses is the headstand or *inversion*. When the individual is completely vertical with their hips stacked directly over their shoulders, they may briefly feel weightless. With weightlessness can come fear, disorientation, and vulnerability. Partnering explorations mimic a similar fear, in that partners will at times completely absorb another dancer's weight. This exciting physical edge can be met with healthy communication tactics and body–mind centering. To explore their physical edges, dancers often use the stability of a wall or spot. In both yoga and partnering, the presence of another person provides safer opportunities to try new explorations, poses, and complexities.

Once a dancer feels the full weight of another and recognizes their capacity to support others, promoting self-care becomes an avenue for making the strong connections, freedoms, and risk-taking associated with partnering. Additionally, career longevity and efficiency in dance can derive from the comradery birthed in partnering contexts. Therefore, continued learning of self-care is essential. To become a good partner, dancers seek outlets for bodily care, including somatic practices that guide them in constructive rest, trigger-point work, foam rolling, and embodied anatomical knowledge. Focused attention and awareness are essential in the formation and continuation of positive, effective partnerships. It is not uncommon to see students truly embrace self-care when casted in duet and group work. When students begin to study and practice partnering, watch for synergy even in no-touch connections where partnering is not the emphasis. For example, when a dancer goes across the floor in the grand allegro, the timing and sense of connection to another dancer even when dancing apart will be heightened and amplified.

In many practical implications and exercises within dance education, common themes of touch and support are essential. Teachers can guide dancers into a community where peer-to-peer massage might be a weekly ritual. Some dancers might find that their physical well-being requires professional body work and therapy. Because accountability is emphasized in partnered scenarios, dancers can be empowered by their peers; the benefits of a partnering practice to dancers' overall commitment can be wonderful to witness.

## Embodied Learning: Breath Work—Sensing, Expanding, and Fulfilling

A common element in dancing and dance training practices that is often overlooked and widely underused is the power and potential of the breath to support and expand a dancer's movement. Full and nuanced use of the breath is powerful in embodied practice but is often relegated to yoga or somatics or to coaching of repertory in performance contexts. The use of breath to support, instigate, and calibrate movement is common in many physical practices rooted in Eastern arts and culture. In dedicated yoga practice, development and lengthening of the breath is known as pranayama (Desikachar 1995). In martial arts forms, such as Beijing opera, tai chi, qigong, yoga, and meditation, breathing leads movement. If one can tap into the full potential of breath support and nuanced connection of breath and movement, they reap the added benefits of greater efficiency, injury prevention, cardiovascular ease, and quality-rich artistry (Desikachar 1995). Clarity in the use of breath also serves as a potential unifier when used strategically in duet or group partnering contexts. When dancers can synchronize and even learn to read the cycle of another dancer's breathing, their connective potential is heightened and organic and imparts ease and sophistication in partnered movement.

The following exercises are based on somatic practices that can serve to expand the muscle of the breath. They allow dancers access the full potential of their breath capacity and increase awareness and intentional use of breathing in their practice and performance.

### Alternate Nostril Breathing

Alternate nostril breathing (Nāḍī śodhana) comes from yoga pranayama practices and serves to cleanse the lungs of stale air. This practice is a great starting point for those new to breath work and is also an excellent way to increase understanding of how to control one's breathing (Desikachar 1995). Alternate nostril breathing takes coordination but once students find a rhythm and flow, this practice helps settle the nervous system, calm anxiety, improve grounding, and cleanse the lungs.

Take a comfortable seat, checking for alignment and good neutral posture. Good postures to try include kneeling on the shins while sitting back on the feet, sitting in a cross-legged position, or sitting with the feet out in front. Instruct students to complete one cycle of alternate nostril breathing as follows:

1. Place your left hand on your leg or knee to feel a stronger connection to the ground through your lower body.
2. Exhale deeply and completely. Bring your right hand up to your face. Place your right thumb on your right nostril and inhale deeply through your left nostril.
3. Close your left nostril with your fingers (usually the middle and ring fingers work best). Release your thumb from your right nostril and exhale through the right nostril.
4. Maintain your fingers closing your left nostril. With your thumb open, inhale through your right nostril.
5. Place your thumb back over your right nostril to close it, and then release your fingers to open your left nostril. Exhale through the left nostril.

Begin again, working with steps 2 to 5. Complete five to six alternate nostril breathing cycles. Then instruct students to lower their right hand to the knee or leg and take a few deep, neutral, double-nostril breaths to reset and return to normal breathing.

## Counted Breath Expansion

Counted breath expansion uses a steady increase of counting (on both the inhale and exhale) to expand breath capacity and train the diaphragm to work to its fullest potential. Guide students to begin with an even, neutral breath and to notice their normal breathing cadence and pace while attempting not to intentionally override it by taking control. Begin with a deep and full exhale, with the instructor counting aloud or students counting silently. Expel all of the breath in the lungs. Figure 3.4 breaks down a counted breath expansion sequence. Start with an inhale for a slow four count, then exhale for the same four-count duration. Inhale once more on the four count and then exhale, evenly extending the count to five. Continue increasing this pattern to tolerance. Over time, breath capacity and control of the pace of inhale and exhale should increase. A great beginning goal is to reach an eight count as the longest cycle. With time and practice, expand the cycle to a 10 or even 12 count.

## Zoned Tactile Breathing

Zoned tactile breathing uses strategic pressure in specific torso areas to help expand the breath capacity in certain lung zones. This exercise also exposes imbalances in the torso and back musculature. When students explore the full range and capacity of breath volume,

---

**FIGURE 3.4**   Counted Breath Expansion Sequence Breakdown

**COUNTED BREATH EXPANSION (COUNTING PATTERN)**

*Inhale 1 - 2 - 3 - 4 | Exhale 1 - 2 - 3 - 4 | Inhale 1 - 2 - 3 - 4 | Exhale 1 - 2 - 3 - 4 - 5*

*Inhale 1 - 2 - 3 - 4 - 5 | Exhale 1 - 2 - 3 - 4 - 5 | Inhale 1 - 2 - 3 - 4 - 5 |*
*Exhale 1 - 2 - 3 - 4 - 5 - 6*

*Inhale 1 - 2 - 3 - 4 - 5 - 6 | Exhale 1 - 2- 3 - 4 - 5 - 6 | Inhale 1 - 2 - 3 - 4 - 5 - 6 |*
*Exhale 1 - 2 - 3 - 4 - 5 - 6 - 7*

*Inhale 1 - 2 - 3 - 4 - 5 - 6 - 7 | Exhale 1 - 2 - 3 - 4 - 5 - 6 - 7 | Inhale 1 - 2 - 3 - 4 - 5 - 6 - 7 |*
*Exhale 1 - 2 - 3 - 4 - 5 - 6 - 7 - 8*

*Inhale 1 - 2 - 3 - 4 - 5 - 6 - 7 - 8 | Exhale 1 - 2 - 3 - 4 - 5 - 6 - 7 - 8 |* **Rest**

the physical input of touch and pressure provides a force against which they can respond. Tension and overdeveloped muscles can bind and restrict breath capacity through the front sides and back of the torso, into the pelvic bowl, and up into the upper rib cage. Early in these somatic explorations, students may become frustrated if they are unable to access some of the ranges being asked of them. As many instructors guiding dance students in any form would do, tactile connection and direction through the hands can be a powerful tool for unlocking less familiar pathways and for engagement and release. The first iteration of this exercise uses self-touch to create a subtle force in specific areas of the torso.

This exercise can be done standing, seated in a chair or on the floor (with easeful upright posture), or even lying on one's back. Varied approaches are illustrated in the photos and video resources that follow. Guide students as follows:

1. *Head and tail:* Place one hand on the top of your head, using medium pressure. Visualize the expansion between the top of your head and your tailbone or pelvic floor. Inhale and lengthen into the spine. Exhale.

2. *Lateral:* Place one hand on each side of your rib cage, using medium pressure toward the midline. Inhale, expanding into your hands to feel lateral (side to side) broadening. Exhale, softening to your midline.

3. *Upper torso (sternum):* Place one hand on your sternum and the back of the other hand high between your shoulder blades. Inhale, breathing into the front and back of your upper torso. Exhale, softening to your midline.

4. *Lower torso (navel):* Place one hand over your navel and the back of your other hand on your lower back or lumbar spine. Inhale, breathing into the front and back of your lower torso. Exhale, softening to your midline.

Modify hand positions as needed, depending on the approach. For example, if the dancer is lying down, the floor can serve as tactile input to the back of the body.

### ▶ ZONED TACTILE BREATHING

Two dancers demonstrate useful postures for practice in this exercise and shift through the hand positions.

### Partnered Zoned Tactile Breathing

The partnered version of the zoned tactile breathing exercise has the same outcomes but allows for greater breath capacity when dancers are not using their own hands or arms for tactile input. It also serves as a great icebreaker in regard to touch, sensitivity, and awareness through hand contact with a partner's body. A standing position works best for this exercise because it offers 360-degree access to body surfaces. To begin, the receptive partner stands tall, with their feet hip-width apart and arms relaxed at their sides.

1. *Top of the head:* The active partner uses medium pressure to stack both hands on top of their partner's head. The active partner relaxes their elbows down toward gravity, allowing their arm weight to give pressured, tactile input to the top of their partner's head. The receptive partner visualizes height and length in the spine and inhales, lengthening into the spine and meeting the pressure of their partner's hands. The receptive partner exhales, maintaining height.

2. *Upper torso (sternum and shoulder blades):* The active partner moves to one side of their partner's body and places one hand respectfully on their partner's upper sternum and the other between the shoulder blades, with medium pressure. The receptive partner breathes into the pressure of the active partner's hands, trying to breathe equally into the front and back of the body. Then the receptive partner

inhales deeply, meeting the pressure of the active partner's hands. The receptive partner exhales back to the midline.

3. *Lower torso (navel and lower back):* The active partner moves one hand respectfully to their partner's navel and the other hand to their partner's lower back, with medium pressure. The receptive partner breathes into the pressure of the active partner's hands, trying to breathe equally into the front and back of the body. Then the receptive partner inhales deeply into the diaphragm, meeting the pressure of the active partner's hands. The receptive partner exhales back to the midline.

4. *Lateral torso (side of the ribs, above the waistline):* The active partner moves behind their partner and places one hand respectfully on each side of the rib cage just above the waistline, with medium pressure. The receptive partner breathes into the pressure of the active partner's hands, trying to breathe laterally into both sides of the body. Then the receptive partner inhales deeply, meeting the pressure of the active partner's hands. The receptive partner exhales back to the midline.

5. *Pelvis grounding:* The active partner places both hands on the upper crest of the back of their partner's pelvis, with medium pressure in and down. The receptive partner feels the grounding of their lower body and tries to breathe height into the upper half of the body. Then the receptive partner inhales deeply into vertical length. The receptive partner exhales, maintaining height.

**▶ PARTNERED ZONED TACTILE BREATHING**

Two dancers demonstrate the standing, partnered version of the tactile breathing exercise, with close up shots of hand positions.

# Practical Skills and Frameworks for Teaching Dance Partnering: Part II

All partnering explorations can dig deeper into the biomechanical fundamentals unique to dance partnering. The most fun aspects of partnering are created through connecting and finding ease within risk. This grouping of exercises emphasizes the understanding and beauty of leverage and momentum, with acknowledgment of what the body can accomplish safely. These exercises build on previous foundational exercises to establish a connection and develop an early understanding of partnering potential.

An overview of the exercises follows:

- Exercise 7, Draping, builds on the supportive function of shelves and ledges, but refers to a released connection to the stable surface by the supported partner.

- Exercise 8, Airplanes, explores the prone support of a partner through the legs and lower body.

- Exercise 9, Redirection and Leverage, introduces momentum and lateral thrust to motivate dynamic lifts and support.

- Exercise 10, Over, Under and Through, explains three different ways to support a partner while traveling in space.

- Exercise 11, Falling and Rocking, outlines the possibilities of using counterbalance and stabilization to support and redirect the fall, or rocking action of a partner in motion.

- Exercise 12, Assisted Inversions, offers a framework for partner support for upside-down, or inverted, actions.

## EXERCISE 7
# DRAPING

### Background

Draping is a combined exploration that relates to and builds on previous exercises. When the stability and horizontal support of shelves and ledges (exercise 6) and the yielding principles in active and passive practice (exercise 3) are used, draping can be a useful skill for seamless transitions and a means to find efficiency. Draping requires one dancer to completely surrender their weight to another. When weight is yielded fully and distributed evenly across the supportive surface of a partner, the draping partner's weight becomes one with that of the supporting partner. If balanced evenly, gravity becomes the grounding tether, and the weight centers of both partners are unified. Draping can be connected with exercise 6, Shelves and Ledges, as opposite sides of a coin. Draping specifically attends to the technique of the supported partner.

### Purpose

Draping is a key part of surrendering and allowing weight to pass from oneself to others. In many ways, draping imparts a sense of weightlessness to the viewer. Ease, flow, and follow-through can be traced to effective draping. Like most moments of surrender and ease, students must be guided in the art of releasing, trusting, and allocating weight.

### Foundational Exercises

#### GUIDED IMPROVISATION

One way to play with draping is to use words and images that evoke the idea of surrender. To invigorate an improvisation or partnering practice, draping can be explored and articulated with verbs such as *enclose, cover, drop, suspend, submit,* and *relinquish.* As with many other entry points into a given exercise, allowing students to first practice individually builds confidence for later connection with a partner.

### In Practice: Draping

Objective: To practice submitting and receiving weight through the act of a carry.

#### TABLECLOTH

This safe, low-stakes exploration allows students to discover the feel of draping. The supportive partner offers the broad ledge of the back of their body, using their hands and knees as a four-point base of support. This is also known as the table-top position, as described in exercise 6, Shelves and Ledges. I often encourage students to keep their feet long or tuck their toes under, depending on the shape of the bones in their knee and upper tibia. Maintaining soft elbows and hip joints allows for give when they begin to support a partner's full weight in this position. With partner B in the table-top position, partner A can explore draping over the broad support of partner B's back. Partner A should ease their weight onto their base and then balance their upper and lower body weight on either side, like a tablecloth draped evenly over a table. They can roll, slide, and explore the best positions to find ease, balance, and full yield of their weight, with the most stable zones at the upper back (over the support of the arms) and the pelvis (over the support of the femurs). Beginning this exploration at a low level helps students gain confidence in and understanding of the principles of yielding and balance before they attempt the skill at a higher level.

### SACK OF FLOUR

Instruct partner A to fold over the top of partner B's shoulders, with partner B standing in a wide position. Partner A practices releasing their weight over partner B while partner B supports partner A. The act of draping causes both parties to clarify acts of support and surrender at the point of contact. It is important for students to warm up and engage their core muscles for safety and support through the torso. Remind students to use a deep plié and their leg strength when taking their partner's weight and lifting them.

Like shelves and ledges, sack of flour uses passive draping of the supported partner over the stable, upright base of a standing supportive partner.

## Modifications and Problem-Solving

It can be overwhelming for students to surrender weight over a ledge, with 100 percent of their weight being transferred to their partner. By practicing surrender individually, dancers tend to find the courage to explore it with a partner. If students are reluctant and find it hard to yield their full weight, consider using furniture as a supportive surface to begin. Exploration by draping over a chair, bench, table, or sturdy freestanding ballet barre can help students connect with the concept before working together. It may be helpful to pair students; have one explore draping with the furniture base, while the other functions as a spotter. While spotting for their partner, students have the added benefit of observing creative ideas and problem-solving before they try the exercise.

## Expanding and Advanced Skills

Draping takes on a new level when rotation on the transverse (horizontal) plane is explored. By folding and finding new ledges with circular momentum, new points of draping can occur. Draping with a circular pathway can create momentum and shared points of entry and exit. Related to the action of a hip ride (exercise 13 in chapter 4), the upper leg in flexion at a 90-degree angle relative to the torso can become a stable but mobile surface for exploration of draping with rotation and momentum. Whereas previous examples of draping have a more stable beginning, this advanced version requires clear entry into and exit out of the action. This is a great opportunity to explore communication and problem-solving work, because students are asked to apply previously understood skills to a more challenging version of the exercise.

▶ EXPLORING DRAPING

Students pour and spill over stable supportive surfaces of their partner. This action is related to shelves and ledges but is more yielding, with weight dispersed and released rather than held.

EXERCISE 8
## AIRPLANES

### Background

By understanding the power of the lower body in a conditioning sense, students learn how its large and powerful muscle groups can support the flight and entire weight of another person. In airplanes, the legs possess potential energy to push and yield, eventually combining with a rocking motion to produce efficiency in and out of the motion. When dancers lie supine on the floor, they gain possibility and freedom in the lower body; therefore, their legs mimic the function of their arms and their feet can act as hands. As stabilizers, one dancer's upper legs push and guide their partner's weight. Creating a safe and trusting base of support can be achieved with the legs acting as a stable and mobilizing foundation and the back of the body serving as the beginning of that foundation.

### Purpose

Airplanes explore the function and power of the legs. Just as the arms and hands grasp and clasp, an airplane exercise can be used to begin exploring how the legs can help steer and provide opportunities for horizontal flight. As students begin to understand giving and receiving weight, airplanes provide an exciting opportunity for their limbs to play a role.

### ▶ AIRPLANE DEMONSTRATION

Students demonstrate proper entry into and exit out of airplane-style support. Variations are offered, with the supported dancer connecting in different ways.

### Foundational Exercises

#### CHOO-CHOO TRAIN

Just as a train moves on a track, this foundational exercise connects through the transverse plane as the left foot of partner A's foot makes contact with partner B's right foot and partner A's right foot with partner B's left. To help dancers safely explore the power of the legs in a nonvertical position, have them bend their legs in tandem with one another, like a train moving back and forth, while keeping the foot-to-foot connection. Because the lower body is built to mobilize, experimenting with the sensitivity and nuance within this region takes skill (e.g., think back to learning to drive and tapping the gas and break). Dancers quickly learn that the legs can find nuance when it comes to pressure and control.

#### FOOTHOLDS

How can the feet, as a system of support, hold space? With footholds, dancers explore walking along or up a partner. Have students consider questions like these: What areas of the feet connect to vertical spaces? How do you receive the floor without your feet as the main source of connection? In other words, how can the lower body, particularly the lower leg, act as the hands? Similar to how the feet assert verticality, the legs become a stable force with which to support a partner. By exploring a nontraditional improvisational prompt in which weight is received via the lower body, one partner can use their feet to hold a fellow dancer.

### In Practice: Airplanes

Objective: To explore how the lower body plays a supportive role when it is free to mobilize and direct energy and to use different planar relationships of the torso to floor to show how legs can function as arms.

Partner A lies supine on the floor, extending their arms and legs upward toward the ceiling. Partner B stands at the base of partner A. Through eye contact and proximity, partner A bends their legs while partner B presses of their hips forward; this causes partner A's feet to meet the front of partner B's pelvis. Partner A receives partner B's weight with thoughtful resistance and through a bend in the legs. Through this bend, partner B can reach for partner A's hands. Review exercise 1, Grasp and Clasp, in chapter 2. Partner B pushes off, and partner A receives the force and weight of the rock. Partner B stacks over top of partner A, hand to hand and foot to pelvis. For beginning dancers, partner B's legs often try to maintain connection to the floor. As their confidence increases, partner B can reach their legs in line with their horizontal pelvis.

Example airplane positions with partner A (on the floor) supporting partner B (in flight).

## Modifications and Problem-Solving

In airplanes, partner B can easily break at the hips, which results in a disingenuous connection between partner A's foot and partner B's pelvis. In other words, partner B is not giving their weight forward to partner A. Partner B must think of planking for a moment as they are rocked into the airplane position. Partner A must avoid locking the legs to support partner B's weight. The legs can activate, but avoid the damaging effect of going beyond a 180-degree extension. Note that partner B may be startled and tense up when they experience the thrill of going off the ground with all limbs connected to partner A. If tension and locking continue, return to the foundational exercises where exchange is along the floor.

## Expanding and Advanced Skills

Experimenting with asymmetrical variations of airplanes naturally creates great transitions. As partner B goes into flight, partner A can aid in redirecting partner B in myriad directions. As their confidence builds, partner B can extend their spine and arch, giving into a reverse c curve. Once partner B is confident in flying and partner A in supporting, the rocking descent of the flight is a great way to recycle energy and reverse roles. Partner B pulls partner A to their feet, contracting to the floor and becoming the new base of support for partner A to take flight.

## EXERCISE 9
# REDIRECTION AND LEVERAGE

### Background

The study of redirection and leverage can begin later in partnering practice when dancers have developed their responsiveness and quick reactions and have studied previous explorations (e.g., exercise 1, Grasp and Clasp; exercise 3, Active and Passive; and exercise 6, Shelves and Ledges). Note for students that redirection is observed in everyday movement, such as when a parent redirects a child's hand or travel pattern or an usher gestures an individual to take a different path. They become instant problem-solvers by using their body and weight to redirect and act as a lever. The root of redirection and leverage is looking and listening for opportunities to redirect a partner or be redirected. Redirection uses the pathway and momentum of a partner to send them in an opposite or alternate trajectory.

Leverage is the act of allocating where weight and counterbalances exist within the play and partnership. The action of a lever requires a stable fulcrum or pivot point; in a dance context, this could be the base of support in connection with the ground or a part of the body space holding as another part is mobilized.

This is redirection in action. Partners demonstrate the dynamic outcome at the peak of a redirected lift achieved by using momentum and centripetal force.

### Purpose

The ability to play in redirection and leverage is key to exploring a partnership. Because no two partnerships are alike, redirection and leverage allow dancers to problem-solve in the moment. Ask students to consider questions like these: What if your current partner has a much lower center of gravity? What if your current partner really uses a lot of momentum in this transition? How can you anchor or guide the connection elsewhere? Redirection and leverage also allow for unpredictable partnered connections from the audience's point of view. Redirecting where energy goes is one of the most exciting parts of movement exploration. For example, repurposed energy is vital in harnessing and redirecting a jump that may lean back.

### Foundational Exercises

#### GUIDED IMPROVISATION

Begin with students dancing alone. Have them locomote through the space, gradually increasing speed as they go. The perimeter of the space, objects in the room, or other dancers might serve as stopping points for dancers to set one foot and quickly change direction. The shift of direction might be a full redirection to where they came from or set them on a new angle or path through the space. Key aspects for students to sense as they explore include (1) the stable pivot point of the point they redirect from and (2) the shift in momentum toward a new direction.

#### WORKSHOPPING

Redirection and leverage can occur in any partnered connection. For example, students can explore redirection by repeating and reinventing any exercise, choreographed moment, or image and reframing it through different entry points and exits.

Explore together through improvisation. Have students move through the space at a moderate pace. When an opportunity arises, they might choose to interject, connect to another dancer, and use their momentum to take a new path. Without resorting to shoving or slinging the other dancer, students find a soft connection, go with the partner they are directing to feel their trajectory, set one or both feet, and use a connection through the hands or arms to interrupt their pathway.

▶ REDIRECTION AND LEVERAGE

Students demonstrate back-swing with a horizontal redirection.

### In Practice: Redirection and Leverage

Objective: To explore the dynamics of redirection of a partner's momentum along a new pathway, using leverage for redirections along the horizontal or vertical planes. By exploring different redirection and leverage mechanics, students hone sensitivity, responsiveness, and intuitive use of drive.

### U-TURN

Organize students in pairs, with the supportive partner (partner A) on one side of the room and the supported partner (partner B) on the other. Ensure that each pair has their own lane. Partner A serves as a stable fulcrum or point of rotation, and partner B accesses momentum to move around partner A.

For a safe and simple version of this lift, partners use a side-by-side connection moving through a stag leap–style jeté with partner B's front leg bent and the back leg trailing long. The upper body connection should be such that partner B's arm closest to partner A wraps high around the sternum and the outside shoulder. Partner A should wrap their inside arm around partner B's waist. Partner A can then use their outside hand to press against partner B's mid-back, just under the shelf of the shoulder blade.

Students should find this connection and arm placement before they explore the full expression of the jump and redirection. Once the connection is clear and mapped, partner B can reset farther back from partner A and prepare the run. While running forward toward their partner to build momentum, partner B should wrap their arm as they take off from their outside leg into the stag leap shape. Although partner B will be redirected around the corner, they should maintain a sense of linear trajectory up and through as if to jump past their partner. A helpful placement for the lower body is for the supported partner B to try and jump high enough while moving forward, to get their pelvis above the outside of partner A's hip. The hip can then become a shelf to take some of their body weight.

As this action is happening, partner A should wrap their inside arm around partner B's waist and, without gripping, pull their partner's body weight toward their own torso to connect both of their weight centers. Using the momentum generated by partner B's run and jump, partner A should set their outside foot and pivot around and away from it 180 degrees. The forward momentum assists in the rotation around the stable, planted foot and redirects partner B back in the direction they came from.

▶ U-TURN REDIRECTION LIFT

Partner B performs a running leap and then partner A lifts and redirects partner B 180 degrees.

To help students understand both sides of the action, have each partner try both roles and then switch. Have students discuss what they discovered in their practice of the first role. Sharing information empowers growth in the moment and more efficient exploration of the opposite role in the exercise. Once students become comfortable with the mechanics of redirection, explore different connections and shapes to jump and redirect. As they workshop new ideas, encourage clear communication and up-front discussion of the connection that will be used. As students advance within this practice, more improvisation and free exploration can be encouraged. Once they learn to quickly read the pathway and preparatory takeoff of their partner, intuitive reactions can emerge within this action.

*> continued*

## BACKWARD FLIGHT

Although backward flight is still a redirection, the principle of leverage is also clearly used when redirecting the supported partner back in the linear pathway they came from.

With the same setup as the U-turn redirection that uses a circular pathway and centripetal force for efficient redirection, backward flight can also start with running momentum of the supported partner (partner B) toward the supportive partner (partner A). A pelvis-to-shoulder connection is a safe and excellent way to begin exploration of backward flight. By using a stable two-directional plié, partner A receives partner B's weight with their dominant shoulder connecting to the low front pelvis of partner B. For partner B, the setup action will feel like a temps levé or temps de fleche, and they should take care to jump high enough to get slightly above partner A's receptive shoulder as if to jump up and past them. The forward momentum paired with a stable connection then allows partner A to drive forward and use the trajectory of partner B to lift them and smoothly travel backward toward the starting point.

## ▶ BACKWARD FLIGHT LIFT

Backward flight lift is demonstrated alone and connected to a U-turn redirection.

### Modifications and Problem-Solving

The most common challenges that students experience when exploring redirection and leverage are hesitation and loss of force or momentum, unstable grip and disconnection between partners' weight centers, and inefficient or less functional footwork and use of weight transfer, pivot, or revolution.

For unclear upper body connection and arm placement issues, have students stop, slow down, and practice the entrance into the position that will be used. This is a great opportunity to communicate and fine-tune according to a given partner's stature, weight center, and comfort level. Like going in for a slow-motion hug, the upper body pathway can be practiced on its own and then connected with the jump and lower body action once it is clearer between partners.

Similarly, problems with footwork and weight transfer can be practiced by the supportive partner (partner A) on their own first. Once the connection, jumping action, and direction of rotation are established, partner A can practice the weight shift and stable rotation around a supporting leg, maintaining soft, malleable knees and ankles and paying attention to foot rotation. When the lower body action is clear, partner A then practices the timing of their step pattern along with the takeoff and trajectory of partner B.

### Expanding and Advanced Skills

To deepen exploration of redirection and leverage, students can work toward a fuller improvisational approach to the exercise. By honing adaptive responsiveness, sensitivity, and intuition, both partners can trade roles within the same practice. Partners can read their trajectories and preparation for jumps and leaps to take on the supportive and supported roles more freely and reflexively. Creative ways to set up and connect with a partner can also increase the level of difficulty and, in turn, the payoff of increased skills and technical mechanics.

Another way to deepen and challenge practice is by increasing the height of lifts into the press lift range at or above shoulder level. Like the famous "bird" lift in *Dirty Dancing* (1987), press lifts can also function in the leverage aspect of redirection lifts.

Once explored and understood, redirection and leverage exercises can be combined with the principles in exercise 10, Over, Under, and Through. With a traditional jumping takeoff, the base exploration is most like the over action; by adding a glide or sweep and swing, the under and through actions can also function within a supported redirection lift.

To help students gain confidence, begin at a closer range with less force and drive in the action of supported partner B. By reducing momentum and, by extension, risk, students can experience harnessing a partner's pathway at a lower intensity. They can then build up speed, force, and distance between partners at the setup of the exercise.

## EXERCISE 10
# OVER, UNDER, AND THROUGH

### Background

Within the realm of supported traveling lifts, a common approach stems from traditional classical ballet mechanics in which momentum is used at first but quickly gives way to the brute strength of the supportive partner in what essentially becomes a carrying lift. With the three different movement potentials of over, under, and through, weight and momentum are used to further the movement by taking an active approach to being supported in a lift. The lifted partner is not simply passive and controlled by the supportive partner; rather, the lifted partner begins an action that their partner further supports. By no means is this intended to suggest that dancers being lifted in classical ballet partnering are not engaging, lifting out of their own weight, and holding their center. Beginning dancers in ballet partnering often lack this understanding of the active role required for successful lifts. Exercise 10 offers a less formal approach to learning these skills, which can then be reapplied to more technical, traditional lifting. In practice, this exercise is most effective when kept in an improvisational mode. Some front-end planning and instructional organization are beneficial, but the opportunity for the unexpected allows students to develop an authentic and responsive awareness to unpredictable force.

### Purpose

This exercise builds strength through repetition and fosters the development of nuance and perceptiveness when approaching an improvised partnering dynamic. Students gain awareness of the useful potential of tapping into a partner's weight to further their movement and begin to understand efficiency in partnering by harnessing momentum and force. Although the three versions of this approach (over, under, and through) use a different relationship to weight and directionality, they have overlapping mechanics that allow students to understand a broad range of ways to support a partner in dynamic traveling lifts.

### Foundational Exercises

#### GUIDED IMPROVISATION

The physical dynamics required in a given partnering principle can be practiced individually before students begin explorations with a partner. Solo exploration is often most effective for developing the patterning of the supported partner in these traveling lifts. With all dancers working in solo exploration, richer understanding of both roles can be achieved. If the instructor is using balanced and inclusive pedagogy (as discussed in chapter 5), students also will benefit from practicing both the supported and supportive roles. To develop advanced skills in this area, roles can overlap and blur to fine-tune responsiveness.

To develop the foundation for a thorough and successful exploration of this exercise, guided improvisation that practices patterning for all three physical dynamics (over, under, and through) is a helpful start. Have students spread out around the room. It can be beneficial to first practice in a contained, multidirectional space and follow that exploration by going across the floor, introducing a more specific trajectory or pathway. By first exploring in an open space, dancers can follow their own physical response to the movement prompt with more opportunities; adding the limitation of a singular pathway to travel can result in creative possibilities to further their exploration of the score.

Each action can be explored on its own and discussed individually to allow students to verbalize and more thoroughly imagine the subtle differences between the three physical dynamics.

#### *Over*

The *over* action can be described as a lofted, upward-sailing arc and is perhaps most related to what is observed in a supported lift in ballet or modern dance partnering. The peak of support by a partner is exerted at the top of an arching jump, such as a grand jeté or pas de chat in ballet partnering. To explore this physicality, simply coach dancers to practice exaggerated,

> continued

long leaps with a very clear entry into and exit out of the jump. This clear and intentional preparation will help later with *broadcasting* the entry into a jump, allowing the lifting or supporting partner to locate and connect with their partner's weight trajectory and to provide support just before and during the peak of a traveling jump. This preparation also provides an opportunity to connect a dancer with their breath by accentuating the inhale on the upper arc of the jump, as if they are levitating, and emphasizing the exhale during the landing and subsequent takeoff into the next leap.

### Under

To explore the *under* action, students use a deep connection to the undercurve. Offer guided prompts to help students access weight and a resilient, buoyant relationship with gravity. The image of a wet mop comes to mind, with the weight of the mop head moving in response to the force and directionality placed on the handle. In this solo exploration, students should imagine this motion in their torso and pelvis in coordination with a smooth, under-curved transfer of weight.

### Through

The *through* physical action, perhaps the most elusive of the three in this exercise, can most easily be described as a slide. With a trajectory that moves horizontally, the feet tend to skim the floor after a very low micro jump. A bound, engaged body center and limbs allow the dancer to move laterally in one piece. With a setup similar to the over action, the upward momentum in the through action is redirected horizontally instead of arching upward. When students fully explore the through action with a partner, the supported partner must create a sense of lift and lightness to the slide but should not overly emphasize the upward action of a typical vertical jump. This often proves to be the most fun and laughter-producing part of the exploration. Students can work on sliding mechanics by creating momentum with two or three running steps, engaging their body with two feet on the ground, and then sliding. This action can be achieved more easily in socks or dance shoes; it can be explored with bare feet, but more friction is inevitable and limits the range of travel. Invite students to check their breath patterning; they should feel the breath catch and hold during the sliding action.

## WORKSHOPPING

### Handshake and Push and Pull

Before students begin to fully connect and explore over, under, and through with a partner, offer a helpful intermediate exercise such as the handshake or the push and pull.

Set students up to travel across the floor, with each pair having a set lane. Dancers should face one another, with the leading partner's back pointed in the direction of travel. Dancers then connect their right (or left) hands as in a handshake and soften their legs to prepare for a quick response to force in any direction. The leading dancer with their back to the direction of travel should pull their partner past themself and direct them down the line of travel. The force of the pull, coupled with the following dancer's core engagement and strong connection of arm to core, will allow them to easily pass by and beyond their partner. While first practicing, the momentum can then be interrupted before the dancer who just traveled becomes the one to initiate the next pull of their partner in the same manner. Once students find a rhythm and begin to find the most beneficial preparation of their legs, the transitions between roles can become seamless, with the pull of one dancer and subsequent traveling jump producing the force to drive the next pull while dancers quickly switch roles. This exercise then becomes an exploration of coordination and timing and offers students an opportunity to experience the amount of force needed to move a partner fully past themselves. These dynamics will prove invaluable as students enter the full exploration of exercise 10 with improvised and assisted traveling lifts.

### Grips and Supportive Options

By expanding the base ideas that students explored in the foundational improvisation exercises, a move toward partnered explorations of over, under, and through increase student awareness of these three action trajectories. It is important to discuss the safest and most secure and comfortable grips to use while supporting and lifting a partner before fully exploring this practice.

### Key Ideas to Relay to Students

• Take most of the partner's weight into the palm of the hand rather than connecting with effort in the fingertips. Support through the hands avoids an uncomfortable poking feeling and bruising, and it allows dancers to form a more secure and whole connection with their partner. Lifting or supporting one's partner as if wearing oven mitts is a useful metaphor for broader support with weight distributed evenly across the whole hand.

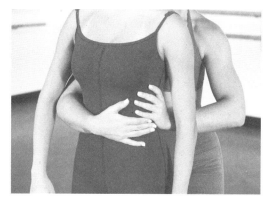

• A perpendicular hold is a secure option beyond the traditional two-hands-on-waist grip. For this type of hold, the supportive partner wraps their dominant arm around the supported partner's waist (like a belt), and the supportive partner's other palm securely holds the opposite side of their partner's body. The supportive partner uses the wrapped arm to pull their partner's weight closer and they use their other palm to stabilize any potential tilting of the supported partner's body. Essentially, the wrapped arm stabilizes front to back and the second hand stabilizes side to side.

In the perpendicular hold for supported partnering, the multidirectional stabilization of the supported partner's body allows the supportive partner to more accurately lift and further their partner's movement and trajectory.

• The underarm hook is a common supportive method, particularly for the under motion. The supportive partner hooks both of their elbows under the supported partner's underarms. As their weight drops, the supported partner draws their forearms in, engaging both the biceps and triceps to support their partner. It is important to encourage the supportive partner to stabilize their shoulder blades down their back to engage their lats and draw in their core to support quick transfer of weight into their arms, which can strain their back if not engaged properly. This method is often used by individuals who have less arm strength because it allows them to stay close to the partner they are lifting, which always allows for a stronger connection.

Dancers demonstrate the underarm hook, a useful option for beginning students.

> continued

- Regardless of the grip or hold used, encourage students to draw their partner's weight toward their own body center. By doing so, the supportive partner can access more strength in their arms, back, core, and legs and find more balance and stability through movements with increased momentum. This balance potential is achieved when the weight centers of both partners are closer together, allowing the weight to be moved as one.

### In Practice: Over, Under, and Through

Objective: To hone awareness and quick responsive connections in improvised traveling support of a partner.

### OVER, UNDER, AND THROUGH

Once the instructor has (1) provided opportunities to build on the solo physical explorations in the foundational exercises and to practice guided improvisations and (2) dedicated time to communicating safe and useful ways to support a partner without hurting them, the dancers are ready for the full exploration of these traveling, improvised lifting dynamics. With a singular direction of travel, organize the exercise to either alternate roles with each new lift or use a lift-and-reset strategy that keeps each student in the same role as they move across the floor.

#### Lift and Reset

In the lift-and-reset option, partner A serves in the supportive role and partner B in the supported role. As partner A sets up next to partner B but farther out into the space, partner B runs toward partner A in preparation for a given exploration (over, under, or through). Partner A lifts and moves partner B across the space. Partner B then holds back as partner A resets farther into the space as they move across the floor. They repeat these actions as space allows. Dancers can switch roles as they come back across the floor in the other direction. As with a traveling phrase in a technique class with students dancing individually, here instructors must also organize the roles within the pairings of dancers as they move across the floor together.

#### Alternating Roles

In this option, partners alternate roles as they cross the floor. This option can be used right away or serve as a step that allows dancers to feel a more advanced version of the exercise. Students might begin with partner A supporting partner B in the first lift and then alternate the setup right away so partner B is supporting partner A in the next connection. By removing the reset used to maintain roles, this option allows for the momentum to continue without cutting off the flow and drive as dancers travel through space. Although the momentum requires a quicker read-and-react response from the supportive partner, more efficiency can be discovered without a start-and-stop action. With these approaches and others, the instructor can tailor the experience to students' ability and comfort level. If these ideas are very new to dancers, then the lift-and-reset option is a great place to start because it allows students to focus on one role at a time. It also minimizes momentum, which students may find fast if they are still learning to read the trajectory of their partner's path, weight, and preparation and respond with a grip and support that will further the movement in a traveling lift.

#### Over

Of the three dynamics explored in exercise 10, over is a great place to begin. Most dancers think of this first when guided into a traveling lift with a partner. Tap into the ideas in the solo explorations and guide dancers to use a clear undercurve or plié after they take a few running steps to get momentum. The preparation step leading into the jump should occur within arm's reach of their partner (at most) and directly in line with the side of their partner's body that is closest to them. Prepping directly in front of their partner, beyond them, or not close enough into them will not allow the supportive partner to connect, align with their preparation, and accentuate the movement with a lift. Some of these spacing issues will be discovered naturally as dancers begin to explore—with inevitable giggles along the way. Once students are in the groove, this exploration shows them how much awareness and connectivity with another dancer they have developed.

It is important for the instructor to consider the supported partner's presentation of their body, with accessible options for a partner to connect and lift with clear, intentional broadcasting of their momentum and preparatory steps. If the supported partner runs toward the supportive partner but has a small, closed-off body shape (with arms by their sides or folded in and legs long and stiff), there will be few options for their partner to connect with them and support their weight in a lift. It is important for the partner being lifted to present a broad, open body position with a lot of negative space. The supportive partner can then hook under the waist, torso, underarms, and even the knees or hamstrings for more upward leverage in the lift. Likewise, if the supported partner runs toward the supportive partner too quickly and without a clear preparatory step that their partner can read, a disconnect in the upward momentum that creates the over action is inevitable. Clear and broad use of a plié out of running steps is essential.

As partners master the entry into and peak of the lift, it is imperative for the instructor to explain the need to continue supporting and lifting as the supported partner descends back into the floor. As dancers begin this exploration, their loft or lift might be short and only slightly accentuate the jump their partner might do on their own. As their lifts get longer and higher, attention to supporting all the way back into the ground is essential (as discussed in depth in chapter 4 in exercise 15, Traditional Lifts).

### Under

This under exploration might initially feel counterintuitive to dancers as they work to understand the necessary release of weight and fall required to make this action successful and dynamic. In direct opposition to the over exploration, under draws momentum and weighted drive by using a falling action of the supported partner. Described most easily as a heavy, wet-mop effect, the supported partner will fall from a bit of distance (but still within arm's reach) of the supportive partner who then swings them forward into space along the path of travel. The most common grip used for this technique is the underarm hook. The supportive partner will connect with and stabilize the supported partner's upper body and use the swing and weighted dangling of their partner's torso and legs to move them through space. A good way to begin is similar to a trust fall from summer camp icebreakers. Have partner A (in the supported role) stand a bit farther than arm's length away from partner B (the supportive role). By creating space under their arms to provide an opportunity for partner B to hook underneath, partner A falls backward and lets their weight spill downward and toward their partner. As partner B stabilizes their upper body, partner A should continue the sense of falling in the lower body for the first half of the action. There is a critical moment—as partner A passes by the vertical plumb line and center of gravity of partner B—when the supported partner then must re-engage their core to draw their legs up and forward to be ready to take their own weight as they come back to their feet farther across the floor. Practicing with less risk will help partners identify this vital interchange between active and passive use of weight. At first, this action will feel small and simple; with more momentum and running steps into the falling preparation, the movement becomes even more dynamic. Dancers can explore variations by attempting different supportive grips, falling backward or forward into their partner, and varying body position.

It is important to instruct the supportive partners to engage their core to protect their back muscles from the downward action of dropped weight. As the momentum increases or the distance of preparation widens for a more dynamic and risky lift, the potential strain or impact on the back increases. Warm-ups for this class will certainly benefit from the dedicated core-engaging exercises explained earlier in this chapter.

*> continued*

### Through

Through is the most surreal of the three physical dynamics in exercise 10, because the supported partner seems to float or glide as a result of the weightless quality projected. By using a true horizontal motion that eliminates arching upward or downward, the weight of the supported partner is held and maintained by reducing friction on the floor (while still connected to it). Like the action of a hoverboard, the friction-reduced connection to the floor is then motivated out in space in one piece. This action requires the supported partner to fully engage their core muscles and stabilize their distal limbs to achieve the horizontal motion without jumping. In preparation, all action is projected forward in space, glancing just past the supportive partner to eliminate the upward or downward action of the previous options. For this exercise, a useful grip for support involves wrapping the leading arm around the waist of one's partner and using the trailing arm with an underhand grasp (with fingers pointed away) under the armpit or shoulder of the supported partner.

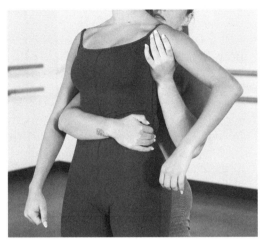

This two-directional supportive grip allows the wrapped arm to draw a partner's weight toward one's own center of gravity, while they use the second arm with an underhand grip to support part of the weight upward.

With this two-directional grip, the supported partner has control of the bulk of their supported partner's weight and draws their centers together. With the supported partner's weight stabilized, that partner then uses a weight shift to continue the horizontal momentum of the supported partner. Keeping the feet stabilized, the supportive partner should begin in a sort of second-position lunge toward their partner (away from the direction of travel); once the grasp is complete, they can shift through second position to their opposite side lunge (along the direction of travel). This is the most basic version of the lift, and it allows the supportive partner to remain grounded and in control of their own weight and that of the supported partner.

More advanced executions of this principle might allow for a low running action by the supportive partner to draw the sliding lift out more. The direction of travel can be less linear by curving or revolving, requiring different preparation, footwork, and weight shift.

### ▶ OVER, UNDER, AND THROUGH

Two partners explore the three dynamics in improvisation format. Textual titles identify the three different options as they are demonstrated.

## Modifications and Problem-Solving

Some students may find the over, under, and through concept intimidating at first, and others may balk at mandated improvisation when they are unsure what to do or where to begin. If students have difficulty starting with improvisation, flip the model and coach them through specific basic versions of each lifting principle. After students understand the mechanics and feeling of each action, they may be more open to and successful in an improvisational context.

Other modifications may be necessary to account for differences in partner height, weight, and stature or to help students simplify the principles if they are less comfortable with supporting a partner's weight in motion. To help students increase their confidence going into the practice, the footwork and weight-shifting mechanics of each lift can be clearly defined and practiced before they take a partner's weight. Often, this clarity of the base of support allows students to approach the improvisational practice more confidently.

The most common problems likely to arise are (1) disconnects based on timing and coordination between partners or (2) unclear preparations by the supported partner that are not easily readable by the supportive partner. For timing issues, set a specific movement to counts or sign the phrasing or rhythm of the steps and action. Music might also help if dancers respond more to music than counts for timing. For problems related to disconnection in preparation, have students slow down or shorten their distance at first to allow for more successful broadcasting of preparation and trajectory. It is common for new partners to need time to learn each other's tendencies before they are able to connect and coalesce more seamlessly. Quicker reading of a partner's tendencies can also be learned over time. Once partners have grasped the exploration and practiced both supportive and supported roles, switch partners to improve adaptability.

## Expanding and Advanced Skills

Keeping these explorations of over, under, and through improvisational allows students to work and practice at their own pace and accomplish the principle relative to their strength, coordination, and confidence at that time. Even within the improvised exercise, students can advance their skills by increasing the scale and distance of travel in any of the three actions, increasing the distance (and risk) of the preparation and takeoff, or adding more force or momentum going into a lift.

Another simple way to increase difficulty is to frame the practice of any of the three lifting principles by having the partners alternate roles as they travel through space. As mentioned earlier, this increases the pace and momentum of the exploration and requires quicker thinking and faster reactions. Similarly, allowing students to overlap the over, under, and through motions without giving their partner notice provides an opportunity for dancers to develop their ability to read the weight and trajectory of their partner. To elongate the exercise, allow students to break from the linear across-the-floor framework and move any direction in space. Expanding possibilities allows for even more spontaneity and changes in direction or arching lift pathways. Stamina is also developed when each round of exploration can last much longer than the short time it may take to cross the dance floor and wait for the next turn to cross.

# FALLING AND ROCKING

## Background

Like the plié is a commencing action in every major turn or jump, falling and rocking is a fundamental part of many contemporary partnering connections. The movement must start somewhere. Falling results from reaching for something and either overshooting or undershooting, whereas rocking involves gently moving back and forth, as in soothing an infant. Whether in a takeoff or descent, the ability to transfer energy by rocking or falling can be seen everywhere. Both actions require bending and suppleness. The sheer actions of falling and rocking ensure momentum exchange, play, thrill, and efficiency. When amplified, falling and rocking can leave viewers speechless. In considering weight and how dancers dig and root themselves into the ground, falling and rocking is a skill in and of itself.

## Purpose

Falling and rocking emphasize the transfer of weight and tension in myriad settings. Free falling is exciting in live modern and contemporary dance. Adding a partner to the mix can result in additional external forces to negotiate and play with. Falling and rocking can require the art of letting go or surrendering bodily control, and this skill requires nuance and communication in partnering contexts. Weight sharing (discussed in chapter 2) is essential to falling and rocking. However, falling and rocking comprise their own exercise, because the art of passing and receiving energy can result in locomotion and stimulate new opportunities. Just as a dancer must learn to mold into the floor from a vertical position, falling and rocking require malleability and constant curiosity with time, space, and energy. Teachers and students are encouraged to apply their knowledge about the body to falling and rocking. Available, supple bodies respond better to these connections, whereas tight or unyielding bodies are not able to reap the benefits of the transitions and play associated with falling and rocking.

## Foundational Exercises

### ROCKING CHAIR

Partner A sits on the ground and acts as a chair for partner B who is sitting in front of them. Partner A wraps their arms around partner B and rocks them. Because both dancers are sitting on the floor, the stakes are low and can lead to other explorations such as redirection and leverage, active and passive, and rolling points. Remind the dancing pair that rocking is an essential part of human upbringing. Similar to a caretaker rocking a child in distress, students can soothe and redirect energy in rocking. In many ways, falling and rocking can bond the community of dancers. Falling and rocking as a rocking chair can be difficult for students who are unfamiliar with the amount of surface area involved within that physical contact.

### ▶ ROCKING CHAIR IMPROVISATION

Dancers explore leverage, active and passive, and rolling points. Partners switch roles.

### FIST TO FEATHER

This exercise allows students to practice letting someone steer momentum and energy. Partner A makes a fist, partner B tries to move the fist through space, and partner A resists. The dancers repeat this reciprocal tension with various body areas. Partner A pretends their hand is a feather, partner B tries to guide the feather through space, and partner A picks up the energy and guidance of partner B. They repeat this action with other body areas. Have students alternate between a fist and a feather, and ask these questions: Which is easier to rock or guide through space? How does a feather fall?

## In Practice: Falling and Rocking

Objective: To ensure that dancers bring an understanding of weight and tension to the transfer of energy through the actions of falling and rocking.

Partners A and B embrace in a tight connection that can change in terms of the amount of contact (e.g., hand to hand, full hug). The idea is for partners to share the ebb and flow of shifting to prepare for falling. Beginning with the legs, the dancers maintain an embrace and explore one of the following options:

1. descending, falling to the floor, and taking turns supporting their partner's fall;

2. rocking to a new connection, counterbalance, or lift; or

3. forming a large group in which one dancer is rocked while the others catch and receive weight that occurs with falling and rocking.

Students demonstrate the embrace, a useful physical connection to sense the weight of a partner in a rocking action.

In falling and rocking, each dancer must determine how to stay connected while surrendering into the floor. Remind students to avoid locking their legs. Rocking redirects the fall and flow into new connections. Working with a wide base with active knee flexion is key to avoiding lower back strain. The point of connection, such as a hug or hands on the waist, can differ. Note that rocking occurs with dancers acknowledging support and weight. Falling and rocking are tied inevitably to timing. Catching a partner at the bottom of a fall or rock can mean the difference in where the momentum can transfer or carry.

## ▶ FALLING AND ROCKING

Dancers demonstrate falling and rocking actions in partnership, using gravity and counterbalance for ease and fluidity.

### Modifications and Problem-Solving

As discussed in previous exercises, surrendering is a process. The degree of tension in falling and rocking is its form of surrendering through the body. Tempo plays a role in how falling and rocking may lead to new connections. The ability for a continuous wave from one dancer to another can be a by-product of seamless falling and rocking. Dancers can often lead with the neck or upper body, leaving their lower body behind. Because falling and rocking require problem-solving in the moment, it is important to warm up the entire body.

### Expanding and Advanced Skills

Varying degrees of momentum increase the possibilities associated with falling and rocking. Tumbling, cascading, and throwing oneself in the space with another person require bodily thinking and listening. Spatial distance into partnered falling and rocking influences the degree of difficulty. Likewise, the actual speed of rocking and falling informs the connection. Isolation of falling and rocking can make for unique choreographic chances. Falling and rocking are essential in many of the connections explored in this book, including airplanes, assisted inversions, hip rides, traditional lifts, and Me scores.

## EXERCISE 12
# ASSISTED INVERSIONS

### Background

Going upside down can be exhilarating. As the study of modern and contemporary dance shows, the torso does not always need to be fixed over top of the legs. In fact, the legs can be stacked over the torso, with the arms acting as a foundation. Inverting the torso under the legs can bring a rush of energy to the upper body, and many partnering explorations can result from the arms becoming the support system and taking weight.

Beyond the partnering classroom, teaching inversions is often achieved with assistance. Similar to how yoga teachers take students to the wall to study headstands and handstands, dance partnering teachers can lead explorations that remind students that the axial skeleton can be stacked from the feet down to the top of the head. As discussed in previous chapters, the hands are communication devices that feel, sense, reach, grasp, and push. Assisted inversions provide an opportunity for one partner to push into the floor while the other partner grasps and guides.

▶ ASSISTED INVERSIONS

Partners demonstrate successful and safe assisted inversions with intentional preparation into and out of the connection.

### Purpose

Assisted inversions emphasize assisting and supporting a moving dancer. Similar to a partner assisting in the revolutions of a partnered pirouette, assisted inversions have one mobilizing-oriented dancer and one stabilizing-oriented dancer. Because the roles are clear in assisted inversions (i.e., one person helps guide the other into an inverted play with gravity), this exercise becomes the foundation for choreographic exploration and variation.

Overall, assisted inversions require students to understand (1) that the body can stack in interesting ways and (2) that partners can help one another stack and organize. Because guiding the inversion of the head over the tail stands as a foreground for many variations of inverted play and connection, watch for how students attempt this exercise. Attempts at assisted inversion reveal how students might connect not only with their partner but also with the floor. How dancers treat the floor is often similar to how they connect with partners. As dancers go in and out of the floor, falling and rocking and active and passive exercises can support assisted inversions.

### Foundational Exercises

#### PIKE AND HIKE (WITHOUT A PARTNER)

Hiking the hips over the head can be a low-stakes inverted play that coordinates the bottom over the head. By going to all fours and then walking the feet closer to the hands, a dancer can bounce and turn that pulse into a push and pike where the legs stretch. If the dancer drops their head with their face looking toward the wall behind them, the hips stack over the head. This initial pike is a great way to ignite that inverted sensation without a partner.

#### HIKE AND STACK

Hiking the hips over the top of the head can be easy for some students and harder for others. By standing in front of their hiked setup with bent legs and arms ready, partner B can reach for the hip crease of partner A and guide the hiking dancer's hips over their head.

Students demonstrate the support of a partner in assisted inversions with hips over the head.

### In Practice: Assisted Inversions

Objective: To assist or be assisted in inverting the body.

In assisted inversions, partner A stands in a wide position (parallel fourth position) with one leg forward and one leg back. Partner A can be in a double lunge with both legs bent. Partner B is in a calculated distance from partner A so when they go into a handstand, their hands are on the inside of partner A's front foot. After the dancers workshop the distance, the assisted inversion occurs when partner B goes into a handstand near partner A in the lunge. Partner A aids in the inversion by readying themselves to catch and guide partner B's legs toward them along the plumb line of partner B. This is why the appropriate amount of distance is necessary.

> continued

**ASSISTED INVERSIONS > *continued***

Ideally, when the person is fully in the handstand with the top of their head toward the floor, both partners share and feel their center of gravity without shifting their footing.

## Modifications and Problem-Solving

Being upside down can be overwhelming for dancers. However, having a partner nearby with a grounded base ready to assist increases their bravery. Conversely, going upside down near a partner can make dancers feel cautious. Calling on the generous bend in the legs, organizing stable connections to the floor is essential in the supportive role in assisted inversions. Hand–eye coordination and teamwork are also needed for effective, fun exploration. In their first attempts at assisted aversions, students will want to grab their partner's legs immediately. However, as the legs come closer to them, the student must avoid leaning forward—going in the line of force. By maintaining a mobile stacked spine with their arms in front of their chest, the student can receive the momentum of the legs. By not fishing for their partner's legs, the dancer is more likely to have responsive arms to protect their face and forge momentum into a mode of support. When the dancer reaches and guides the legs in, they incorporate the body not just from the shoulder. Remind students to avoid beginning from a static place and articulating the fingernails out. Open, wide palms can receive the leg. For dancers going into the inversion, allocation of hand momentum is important; too little and they will not reach their partner, too much and they can forcefully hit the standing partner.

## Expanding and Advanced Skills

This assistance eventually becomes efficient and comfortable. Partner B, the dancer performing the handstand, can link one arm around the front leg of partner A and try a one-handed handstand. Another variation includes having the ledge of partner B's shoulder girdle resting on the front leg of partner A. Finding points to connect with and support a partner in an inversion without the grip of the hands allows for more transitional movement possibilities by moving in and out of these positions. Mobilizing assisted inversions in phrase work with transitions increases both the challenge and mobilization of the skill.

## SUMMARY

Chapter 3 focused on biomechanical, cross-training, and injury prevention techniques to prepare and support students in the study of dance partnering. The warm-ups and training sequences offered may be useful for preparing dancers' bodies before delving into the exercises and explorations of a particular class. Sequences focused on training the body can also serve as homework for students with gaps and imbalances in strength. Breath work and body care can also serve to maintain and rejuvenate sore bodies after taxing dance partnering work. The exercises in part II of the Practical Skills and Frameworks for Teaching Dance Partnering series focused on reliability while supporting the full weight of a partner, increased momentum and force, and inversions. These skills build on the simpler explorations in part I to increase complexity. For more details and visual references, see the ancillary materials and resources linked to chapter 3 in HK*Propel*.

In chapter 4, Energy and Flow: Activating Creativity, the focus of partnering shifts toward the creative practices of choreography and improvisation and offers prompts and examples of how educators might mobilize partnering within these processes.

## DISCUSSION QUESTIONS

1. What do you do to cross-train in preparation for teaching or performing?
2. What forms of training (e.g., yoga, Pilates, weight training, running, cross-fit, Gyrotonic method, etc.) have served you in support of your dance practice?
3. How might you identify and support the individual needs of your students relative to strength imbalances and overall fitness and well-being?

For additional information, see the ancillary materials and resources linked to this chapter in HK*Propel*.

Calder White and Niki Powell in *To Harbor*. Santa Barbara Dance Theater. Choreography by Brandon Whited.

© Fritz Olenberger

# ENERGY AND FLOW: Activating Creativity

## OVERVIEW

One of the greatest rewards associated with dance partnering is the visible play and exchange of energy between dancers. For many audience members, the connection between dancers is one of the most exhilarating and memorable aspects of a performance. This chapter describes how that artistic product is created, while leaning into the idea that some of the most fruitful parts of dance partnership are actually the creative methods and process-based moments that ignite meaningful connection between dancers.

This chapter provides methods for the creative development of partnering by considering these essential questions: How can teachers and choreographers draw inspiration from the connection, community, and partnering that exist in everyday life? How can this ability to recognize partnering everywhere, combined with a deeper understanding of technical skills, forge unique ideas and connections in the choreography? Skilled partnering and its development in choreography require problem-solving and mindful technique balanced with significant play and creative exploration.

### VOCABULARY

| | |
|---|---|
| composition | pluralistic mindset |
| dialogue | practice |
| improvisational score | process |
| laboratory setting | risk-taking |
| movement generation | |

As a dancer and choreographer, I have found that duet and group interactions bring a heightened sense of relationality and meaning making that solo work cannot. Although solo choreography is significant in its own right, it fundamentally lacks the oppositional dynamics, counterpoint, and narrative potential that manifest in duet and group forms. In concert dance, impactful moments of transcendent partnering can be the most memorable when recalling viewership of past performances. Key moments of partnered action contain the power to imprint on the mind. The dramatic peak of an emotionally riveting pas de deux, unbelievably risky and athletic partnering in a contemporary dance piece, or amoeba-like group interactions in modern dance tend to take center stage in the dance aesthetic and emotional recall of a memorable piece of choreography. The energy flow between partners can express a multitude of reflections of human connection. This exchange of energy also radiates between audience and performers forming memories and even visceral, emotional traces.

As a teacher in higher education often called on to teach dance composition, improvisation, and choreography workshops and direct dance concerts, I have witnessed a range of engagement with partnered forms. There is a direct correlation between students with (or without) dedicated partnering training and the number (or lack) of partnered interactions within their choreography. Instructors cannot expect students to connect with and use partnering when they have not had a chance to understand its possibilities and potential or the techniques, skills, and mechanics involved. For students with this knowledge, creativity in the development of partnering becomes another useful tool in their dance composition tool kit. Through application of partnered interaction in their work, students can access deeper communicative potential and create dances that go beyond conventional group dances without partnering.

This chapter discusses how the technical foundations cultivated in the preceding chapters contribute to creative explorations that help budding choreographers find meaningful dancer connections and unlock potential within their work. By describing generative methods that frame and include partnered explorations within creative practice and experimenting with movement invention ideas that encourage partnering at all stages of the choreographic process, this chapter may inspire new ideas in rehearsal and the classroom alike.

# Methods to Support and Incite Partnered Engagement in Creative Practice: Improvisation, Composition, and Independent Choreography Projects

Although dance partnering skills and mechanics may be less familiar to students, the instructor can tap into dancers' innate creativity to develop unique and intentional partnering that supports the overall movement culture or aesthetic of a piece. For beginning students and novice choreographers, cultivating confidence is a vital first step to unlocking creativity.

## Tapping Into Creative Potential

Some choreographers come to rehearsal with preplanned steps, movement patterns, and spatial formations. This preplanning may stem from choreographers' anxiety regarding preparation or their desire to visualize and actualize that vision in the studio. For these choreographers, the addition of partnering is challenging and thus limited, not emphasized, or excluded entirely. When choreographers avoid mapping out an entire product or outcome and center their creative practice on the process, the development of partnering material that links seamlessly to the movement language of a piece is more fruitful. Partnering is complex, requires communication and problem-solving, and takes time to nurture. If instructors foster a culture of exploration, play, and evolution, the bounds of creativity expand toward unexpected and surprising moments that could not be imagined when working alone.

Creative potential enables teachers to create a space where rich conversation, including how they talk and interact with dancers in rehearsal and educational settings, leads to idea making and exploration. When teachers explore a new creative method or process, they may judge their work prematurely when deciding whether a phrase of material or section of choreography is successful, interesting, exciting, or just right. When they follow impulse without immediate justification, step back, and objectively assess their work, they can move beyond habitual, predictable, and conventional choreographic tendencies. Students educated in K-12 settings with a teach-to-the-test approach tend to seek the endgame—that is, they apply the most effort to work that directly affects their grades or assessments. These students tend to experience anxiety and stress and find the open format of creative processes difficult to manage. With a lack of set parameters or guidelines for dance composition study, their creativity can be blocked. Similarly, their tendency toward perfectionism significantly inhibits artistic creative expression. I have had choreography students ask for a checklist of what they should include in their study. Although I develop studies from a particular skill, method, or combination of compositional ideas, it falls well outside of my pedagogy to give students such a list in what should be an open and creative project. In "Redefining the Ideal: Exquisite Imperfection in the Dance Studio," Robin Prichard reframes students' need for perfectionism by identifying common challenges in partnering, improvisation, and technique classes (Prichard 2017). The author provides practical solutions to avoid negative self-talk and self-judgement while students are still in the learning phase. Prichard also encourages readers to avoid risk aversion by changing the goals and reference points during technique practice.

Teachers and creators can increase the time allotted for dialogue, collaboration, and creative exploration within instructional and creative spaces. Creating a laboratory-type setting in rehearsal emphasizes the process, which allows material to evolve and fosters deeper student investment. That pride of contribution within a process and the community of creativity that is cultivated seeps into partnerships. Dancer communication and connection can then become deeper and more effective when creating and executing partnered material in performance. This meaningful bond, often framed as chemistry and instinct between partners who exude an effortless connection, can be developed over time within a partnership or among a group of dancers who find synergy.

With a positive and curious environment, the class becomes a workshop. Participants have equal weight, with the teacher and choreographer serving as a guide. For dancers new to the partnering and creative process, moments where the intended outcome is not achieved can result in interesting or unique partnered interactions. For example, if a hip ride motion (exercise 13) fails to reach its full flight, the way a student rolls off might be interesting and ripe for further exploration. By fostering an environment where dancers can take risks, make mistakes, and celebrate happy accidents, instructors remove the burden of perfection and help students find new ways of moving. With more experienced dancers, a positive and open work environment leads to playfulness and empowers them to make spontaneous decisions and use their heightened responsiveness. In those moments, the choreographer can capitalize on dancer instinct and experience to create seamless and organic partnered movement passages.

Choreographers should watch for artists who possess a natural love of movement. In many ways, these individuals lead the playful, curious space. New connections are made, and the room takes on a productivity that is contagious. Partnering contexts require suggestions, communication, and problem-solving from inside the partnership, but they also benefit from a neutral outside eye to fine-tune the timing and mechanics. When all collaborators are invited and encouraged to engage in the choreographic process, a pluralistic mindset emerges and everyone involved has a voice; this is how teaching partnering as part of an instructor's practice can positively influence pedagogy and creativity overall.

## Improvisation: Composition in the Moment

Relative to curriculum planning, improvisation is an effective course to place at the beginning of a student's journey within a series of courses focused on creative practice. As a technique and performance modality in its own right, improvisation training helps young students tap into a more personal and authentic way of moving that might help them depart from prior training and conventional movement aesthetics. An organizing principle that frames improvisational practice is the development of *movement scores* that become the plan or map of an improvisation. When individuals work in groups and partnerships in dance improvisation, these scores do not dictate what happens within and results from improvisational practice or performance. Rather, movement scores provide an organizing frame for all parties to follow. Learning to respond creatively to the often narrow parameters of an improvisational score can also help students understand that limitations lead to more creative and unique choices. This skill is helpful when students approach the movement generation phase of choreographic practice.

As mentioned in chapter 1, contact improvisation uses a simple movement score: two partners fall into one another toward a single point of connection. Although the skills and techniques that emerge from contact improvisation practice and performance are complex, the root of the score is simple. When a contact improvisation jam becomes too risky, an improviser can return to this simple score to recenter and focus the experience.

Partnered improvisation is another creative tool used to generate material through exploration or as an approach within the performance. Although partnered improvisation can be simplified and experienced by beginning dancers, advanced understanding of its techniques, possibilities, and safe mechanics fosters the most exciting expression of the form. When a partner has developed sensitivity in physical listening, refined their reaction time, and gained understanding of the physical possibilities within partnering, ease and calm can be located within partnered improvisations that outwardly appear risky with drive and momentum.

Improvisation also serves as a pedagogical tool or framework in which students explore a skill or exercise within comfortable boundaries before they learn set material using that technique. Although this approach may seem counterintuitive because students will not have a predetermined phrase of material to learn, improvisation used for simple skills can help students understand the movement within a comfortable range of their current abilities and even find unexpected and creative outcomes. In this pedagogical application, the skill becomes the score for the improvised exploration of the approach. This dynamic is used in many exercises in this book.

To begin the creative process, choreographers approach movement generation in numerous ways. Some choreographers like to generate movement based on narrative and character development, whereas others emphasize movement first and craft material with body-based initiation, exploration of physical dynamics, or authentic movement or improvisation. Put simply, movement generation is the initial step in choreography that develops phrase material that can be further developed in the compositional phase of dance making.

Partnering might enter either phase (or both) of the choreographic process. If a maker develops partnering material first, solo phrases can be transposed from the partnering passage. Conversely, a choreographer might generate partnered phrases by combining or extrapolating on solo phrases of material. The next section outlines both approaches with suggested prompts. The upside is that either approach results in partnering material that shares the same movement language and aesthetics of the remaining material in the dance. When choreographers isolate duet or group partnered interactions from the unpartnered material within a piece, there is often a clear disconnect inside the work and the transition into and out of partnered sections is usually clunky and inorganic. For makers who engage partnering development in multiple phases of both movement generation and compositional processes, there is potential for seamless partnering expression and clarity of movement language in the work.

## Independent Creative Projects

If students engage in dance composition through choreography workshop settings, independent creative projects, or other situations in which they will work on their own and with a group of other dancers, their foundational skills will be vital. There is great responsibility in leading a classroom or rehearsal process, and student choreographers should be encouraged to lead with intention and care.

Students in leadership roles should be mindful of their peers' capabilities and comfort levels and maintain open communication regarding the depth of skills and mechanics of partnering. It is important for student choreographers to provide clear demonstrations and take their time when imaging and practicing a new lift or partnering sequence assessments. When the instructor loses communication channels with dancers or creates a space where students feel embarrassed to speak up, accidents occur and uncomfortable dynamics often arise. A choreographic process managed with open communication and collaboration fosters full class engagement and can be exciting for growth and creative expression.

# Risk-Taking Rooted in Safety-Expanding Skills

Approaching the rehearsal process and classroom space like a workshop can lay the groundwork for out-of-the-box thinking. Risk-taking rooted in safe mechanics and practices is the fuel that moves the field and art of dance forward. This is not to say that instructors should encourage attempts at dangerous partnering or movement ideas for the sake of danger; rather, they should foster a spirit of innovation that often yields the unexpected. Instead of using partnering opportunities as a time to simply recreate lifts or conventional partnering from outside sources, consider how to find the edge of creating for a particular set of students or dancers in classroom and rehearsal settings. To be sure, locating lifts and partnering skills from other makers and practicing them can be important for exploring the possibilities of partnering and building skill sets. Yet even in that mode, the instructor might choose a lift and then push the edge or find new ways to execute it, expand it, or connect different lifts and movements in unique passages.

Teachers and choreographers work with a variety of partners. Working with different frames, statures, and energies means getting to play to the strengths and uniqueness of a particular dancer. Instead of projecting the same expectations onto every duet, pushing the edge might mean something different for each pairing and can engender unique material for each duet. This is how dance truly reflects life. Everyone is different, and each set of individuals working together will have a different expression of relationality and interpersonal dynamics.

Whereas this chapter focuses on engaging dance partnering through the creative process, chapters 2 and 3 explore the technical and practical knowledge of connections, which are a baseline for a deeper practice. At the root of that practice is experimentation. How can a promenade be interesting with acceleration? How might the simplicity of the grasp and clasp (exercise 1) overlap with a hip ride (exercise 13) while changing facings and locomoting through space? Risk-taking is rooted in play. As dancers become more familiar with partnering, the teacher and choreographer can guide dancers toward greater uses of momentum, drive, and weight-bearing or the simplicity of nuance and sensitive interaction.

Inevitably, the teacher or choreographer must notice when a student is ready for the next level of play. Unfortunately, the toggle of growth is messy and nonlinear, and each student progresses at their own pace. Partnering and working with other people can illuminate students' strengths and empower them to try new things. In the visual world of dance, with its high visibility and wide reach via social networks, developing a personal voice is a large part of that risk-taking adventure. From one maker to another, I encourage teachers to help individuals embrace their unique journeys and inspirations and respond to even the most fleeting whims and impulses.

# Movement Invention and Creative Exploration

Much like how instructors approach creative practices in dance, choreography and improvisation with a focus on dance partnering benefit from intentionality and a clear aesthetic point of view. Without dedicated partnering training, many choreographers and directors do not know where to begin or recreate common or conventional sequences of partnered movement. This section offers insights and creative prompts to activate dance partnering within choreographic and improvisational practice and performance.

## Developing Partnered Material

Like the wide range of methods and approaches for choreography in general, many routes can be taken in the generation of partnering. Partnering may develop visually, in which the teacher or choreographer visualizes and imagines connections without bodies in the space. Movement invention and exploration of partnering can evolve from solo work and layer into duet and group forms.

By considering the development of partnered material within the broader scope of the choreographic process, dancers can begin to develop an individual approach to, and use of, partnering in their creative work. When partnering is compartmentalized and developed separate from the movement language of a dance, it does not seem to have a home in the work. By connecting those processes and generating partnering and solo material from the same root movement vocabulary, internal organization and logic can emerge within the landscape of the dance.

## Generative Prompts and Partnered Compositional Methods

The prompts and methods offered here can help get the creativity flowing. Starting can be the hardest part of creating partnering work. As with any practice, invite students to try these methods on their own or in combination; the instructor can adapt and develop their own approach if they are new to choreographing partnering. It is important to remember that experiencing complex partner work and committing to a robust partnering practice can empower students and budding dance artists to engage partnered connections in their own work. Just as individuals are inevitably influenced by the hybrid styles of their past teachers and choreographers, fluency in partnered practice is learned and refined over time.

## Mirroring: Choreographic Variation and Direct Connection

Within dance partnering contexts, teachers can explore the potential of nonverbal exchange. Mirrored connections, in which dancers mirror the action of another, can foster nuanced physical listening and serve as a great icebreaker at the beginning of a semester or master class. For some, the mutual following of another dancer can lead to harmony, groove, and even a state of ecstasy. When both partners are sensitively leading and following at the same time, a Zen state can arise. Allowed enough time to grow into the exploration, two dancers might find themselves unclear who is leading and who is following. Though this length of time may differ depending on the students in question, usually more than five minutes can be significant enough to fall into a true connection.

Communicate positive, open confidence by encouraging students to take the lead and further trust and listen by truly following another person. In a situation in which students or collaborating dancers are asked to make choices and take initiative, it can be refreshing to follow and take on the attributes of a peer dancer. Have students consider these questions: What is it like to be in another dancer's shoes? What are your partner's unique movement dynamics? How does a classmate allocate energy by accessing weight and momentum? Mirroring calls for and develops physical empathy and can prove satisfying and visually pleasing compositionally.

Mirroring another dancer can be simple. One person leads, and another person follows. At the beginning of an exploration, assign specific roles to help dancers acclimate to the exercise, notice which movements and facings are effective, and find the pace that works best within their pairing. As dancers become more comfortable, increase the complexity by encouraging a change of roles within one round of mirroring or even working toward the seamless, mutual lead-and-follow version.

The exploration of mirroring with locomotion can be even more fruitful. Here, partners A and B set up on one side of the class. They face one another as they locomote across the floor, with partner A leading partner B as if they are a mirror reflection. It is important to pay attention to the facing of the leading partner as they move through space. If the leading dancer turns away and the following partner truly mimics that movement, the following partner cannot see what the leading dancer is doing. In this way, mirroring practice can help develop a dancer's ability to project intention and move with clarity and nonverbal legibility. Encourage dancers to pause, adjust the rate of movement, and be kind to the person following. This exercise is a great no-touch experience that is useful for younger student populations or even during peak cold and flu season when direct touch is riskier, relative to community health and well-being.

## Listening and Responding: Toward a Physical Dialogue

Listening and responding can serve as a helpful generative method in choreographic processes focused on communication and meaningful connections between dancers. Even when the movement stems from abstraction and avoids mimicry or pantomime, a movement conversation can emerge that is more rooted in responding to quality, shape, mood, or body attitude. The ability to authentically witness and respond is truly a practice. Preconceived ideas of what is wanted or needed in improvisations can inform but also block the ability to respond. Ask students to think about their everyday conversations: are they truly listening to the other person or thinking ahead to what they will say, how they will respond, or how they have experienced a similar event? A more meaningful connection can emerge when individuals truly listen to each other.

With a reflexive *you go, I go* approach, dancers can embrace being affected by the unknown. By taking turns and having one dancer wait for the other, a beautiful cadence and patience seeps into the process. In a classroom setting, this prompt can be interesting when it begins with pairs and then expands to exploration in trios or within a larger group of dancers. As the number of dancers increases, the sensitivity and listening required increases as well. For students newer to improvisation, listening and responding can be a great way to remove the pressure of having to produce material. The improvised exploration can be witnessed or recorded and later clarified in set material.

In another exercise with students working in pairs, partner A begins dancing while partner B watches. Partner B does not move. Partner A is instructed to improvise and move freely, then freeze in the position or image of their choice. Once partner A is done, partner B must respond to both the final image and the action of their partner. Partner B has no idea what their partner will do, which creates a genuine, immediate response to stimuli. As dancers explore this exercise, it is helpful to refrain from touch. Touch can add another layer of complexity and may restrict the movement potential of the partner as they respond. Once the conversational stop-and-go pattern has been explored, a physical dialogue of sorts can emerge. This is perhaps one of the most beautiful potential exchanges in partnering and improvisation, because one partner cannot predict what the other will do but works to respond authentically in turn.

### Linear Development

Perhaps the most straightforward method for generating partnered dance material (or any movement phrase) is a linear development approach. Starting with a beginning, material is accumulated in sequential order or progresses with the end of one action informing the next. Although the concept seems simple, generating partnered movement in this way is complex. It offers an opportunity to craft a fluid, organic trajectory within the duet form by allowing the momentum or outcome of a given movement to inform what follows. This approach also helps to democratize a partnership by shifting the focus of the action or supportive mechanics between both dancers, allowing for mutual give and take of support. As the work builds, the instructor can focus on the motion of one dancer, craft the support of their partner as secondary, and then shift the focus to the other dancer.

Another way to think about the linear development of partnered material is cause and effect, or *if this, then that* framing. In an incredibly effective example of this method, UK-based choreographer Wayne McGregor gives a TED talk in which he choreographs collaboratively in real time with two dancers in his company (McGregor 2012). Using the structural frame of the architecture of the letters T-E-D in the TED logo, he directs dancers through a technique of suggestion. While working at a rapid-fire pace that prevents his own overthinking or that of the dancers, McGregor uses activating words or directives to quickly craft a duet phrase through linear development. The effect on the audience is palpable as they witness dance being created before their eyes and then performed immediately afterward. Through a focus on building sequence incrementally, McGregor quickly develops set material from a clear inspiration: the TED logo itself.

In this method, the choreographer uses short directives or provocations to cue dancers toward a type of action he imagines. By allowing them to respond, he does not dictate the action, and the dancer develops the movement and has an easier time retaining and connecting movements into the sequence. By alternating actions between partners A and B, mutual agency is created and a sequence begins to flow when actions are overlapped or performed simultaneously. Once the phrase is built, the timing and quality can be refined.

Building on McGregor's example, the choreographer might instruct partner A to take a stable stance. Partner B then uses their partner for leverage for a high leg extension. Partner A lifts the working leg of their partner immediately after it lands. Partner B slashes their arm through the circle created by their leg and their partner's arm. Partner A rotates the entire shape one-and-a-half times, turning themself and their partner. Partner B presses down on their partner's shoulders with two hands. Partner A supports their partner while they plié and sink the whole shape down to the floor.

## Duet From Solo Material

One of my favorite creative methods for pieces that are less narrative and more movement driven involves generating duet material from solo phrase work. This method is effective for choreographing partnered material that relates directly to the movement vocabulary of the piece. I was first introduced to this method while dancing with Steeldance, a company codirected by collaborative choreographers, Teri and Oliver Steele. The Steeles had a seamless way of beginning a work with eight or nine base phrases and developing solo, duet, trio, and group choreography from that root material. I find this working style to be incredibly effective, and I turn to this method often.

The method of generating duet material from solo work can be used in different ways. For example, a *ghosting* approach frames partner A moving with set material and partner B improvising around and alongside the partner they are ghosting. Beginning with improvisation by partner B can help both partners become comfortable with ghosting, as they focus on echoing and responding to movement energies and pathways in the stable movement phrase of partner A or attend to a shape-oriented engagement with negative space. In some performance contexts, allowing these moments to remain improvisational can foster an exciting dynamic of heightened awareness in the partnership. Without the ability to fall back on set material, an authentic, responsive conversation can occur if the dancers are skilled improvisers. If the desire is to set the material, a stop-and-go approach can be the most helpful when crafting material with specificity. Using an accumulation process, partner A can begin the phrase and continue for one or two counts of eight. They can reset to the top, repeat to reinforce the choices, or clarify their relationship and then add a bit more.

Another effective way to create partnered material from solo phrase work is to interface two set phrases. Have partner A begin with phrase 1 and partner B begin with phrase 2. Since both dancers are performing set material, the composition can emerge by having them begin from different starting points, such as back to back, side by side, behind and in front, in close proximity or from a distance moving toward one another, and so on. The phrase itself and the desired relationship between dancers might dictate how the counterpoint between the two phrases is framed.

To develop material that is even more correlated, use the same method but have dancers perform the same phrase. To move beyond unison, partner A can begin at the top of the phrase and partner B can start halfway through and loop back to the beginning of the phrase when their material runs out. In this way, shared actions and movements are echoed within the partnership, but the relationship between dancers is interrupted by time.

This method can use a touchless approach, keeping a slight distance between partners. Even without touch, lifts, or weight-bearing, a meaningful connection emerges from the direct intention of the dancers moving together. For duets with more direct interaction and weight-bearing, locate movements or passages within the phrase that might be furthered by a lift, carry, shelf, or some other skill. Keep a close proximity when colliding the dancers' individual phrases so the opportunities to connect and accentuate movement into partnering will be easier to locate in the development process.

To further increase complexity, try the same method to create trio partnering from solo phrase material. If that seems too complicated at first, generate a duet from solos and then use the same method to collide a solo and a duet to generate a new triangulated interaction for the three dancers.

## *Solo Phrase From Partnered Material*

In direct opposition to generating duet material from separate solo phrases, extract material created for a duet and reframe it as a solo phrase. Have one dancer begin to dance the duet with their partner absent. What movements must be modified? When might the upper body action used in a lift become an unexpected gesture? Like the previous method, creating solo phrases from set duet material fosters the compositional development of movement that directly relates within a shared vocabulary or style.

# Practical Skills and Frameworks for Teaching Dance Partnering: Part III

Part III of practical skill-building exercises builds on the skills presented in parts I and II. Increased awareness, nuance, sensitivity, and confidence allow students to obtain the most benefit from these exercises. The exercises in parts I and II are excellent stepping stones and serve as foundational exercises for part III. Although each exercise in this chapter has a foundational exercise offered as a warm-up or primer for the full expression of the concept, the instructor can revisit exercises from previous chapters to remind students of those fundamentals and provide clear links between differing types of technical skills and mechanics.

An overview of the exercises follows:

- Exercise 13, Hip Rides, introduces dynamic support of a partner through an under-curving, upward rocking motion .
- Exercise 14, Promenade, explores the rotational support of a partner around their vertical plumb line.
- Exercise 15, Traditional Lifts, introduces the mechanics of lifts drawn from ballet partnering—broken down to explore the mechanics behind them.
- Exercise 16, Over, Initiation and Suggestion, explores a low weight connection between partners with one partner initiating the movement of the other through a range of touch dynamics.
- Exercise 17, Rolling Points, outlines the action of round, circular connections between partners, following the flow of contact.
- Exercise 18, Me Score, offers a group exploration through improvisational support of one dancer by the whole group.

## EXERCISE 13

# HIP RIDES

## Background

Hip rides are symmetrical, approachable versions of lifts common in modern dance partnering and contact improvisation. They use leverage and momentum while connecting the weight centers of both partners to move both centers over the base of support of the supportive partner. Broadly described, the action uses a rocking motion to lift and lever one partner into the air after a grounded undercurve preparation. The most basic version described here is a side-by-side, lateral hip ride, in which the sides of the body connect and the supported partner rides up and over the outside standing leg of the supportive partner while resting on the hip and raised thigh of their partner's working leg.

## ▶ HIP RIDES

This video cluster demonstrates the setup and action of basic lateral hip ride, and advanced variations with the same mechanics.

## Purpose

The hip ride lifts described next, and the many possible variations that use the base mechanics of its action, allow for dynamic and impressive partnering and, once understood, are not incredibly difficult and do not require excessive strength. The setup, action, and sequence of events is also a great exercise to build the foundations for many other more challenging partnered lifts and actions. Leverage, momentum, joining of weight centers, proper use of weight transfer, and potential power in the legs are all explored within this series of exercises. Hip ride mechanics serve specifically as a bridge to the exercises in chapter 3 (exercise 9, Redirection and Leverage; exercise 10, Over, Under, and Through; exercise 11, Falling and Rocking; and exercise 12, Assisted Inversions).

For this series of hip ride exercises, I often ask students to "find a partner of a similar stature." This reason for this specific language is discussed further in chapter 5, but it provides a cue that helps find balance between partners without discussing weight or height. Once students have achieved a foundational understanding of the mechanics involved, have them work with different partners to determine the adjustments needed to account for partners of differing statures. Common adjustments are discussed later in the Modifications and Problem-Solving section.

## Foundational Exercises

### SET UP

An excellent warm-up involves guiding students through undercurves as one would in a modern technique class. Create the U shape of the movement. Underscore the importance of a strong, grounded plié on one leg, staying low while shifting weight onto the other leg, and then standing up on the secondary leg while maintaining proper vertical alignment of the pelvis. Work undercurves in second position, moving from side to side, and then in fourth position on both sides, moving from front to back. This simple preparation not only warms up and engages the large leg muscle groups before students lift a partner, but it also reminds students of familiar pathways already present in their training.

### WORKSHOPPING

Before moving into the lifting exercises, it is helpful to workshop the body-to-body connection and grip for lifts. To prepare for the lateral hip ride explored first, each set of partners stands side by side facing the same direction. Partner A (in this moment, practicing for the supportive role) wraps their right arm firmly around partner B's waist (supported role). In turn, partner B

> *continued*

**HIP RIDES > *continued***

wraps their left arm over partner A's shoulder. Partner A then aligns as much of the surface of their right leg to connect with their partner's left leg, connecting their hips and as much of the side of their torsos as possible. Like two sides of a zipper coming together, students then practice taking their partner's weight before lifting them. With their lateral connection maintained by a firm arm wrap, partner A can take a broad weight shift from their right leg over to lunge on their left leg while keeping the right leg long. Without disconnecting their zippered sides, partner B is then taken off balance and drawn slightly over toward their partner's base of support (in this case, the left leg and foot). Have students practice switching roles and trying both sides, alternating the arm wrapping grip relative to the direction of motion and support.

### In Practice: Hip Rides

Objective: To connect weight centers, move as one, and access leverage to motivate one partner off the ground.

### LATERAL HIP RIDE

Using the setup practiced in the workshopping foundational exercise, partner A wraps their arms and connects to partner B as just described. Partner A can begin with weight on their right leg as they lean toward partner B to connect. While they maintain grip and connection between their sides, both partners plié as in the beginning of an undercurve in second position parallel from right to left. Partner A rocks their weight fully to their left leg, moves laterally while maintaining a low plié, and then stands up strong with their hips (and those of their partner) squarely above their left foot, which is now the base of support for both partners. Their right leg wants to slightly soften into a long parallel attitude position, which then becomes a shelf for partner B's lower body. While partner A executes those safe mechanics to level and lift partner B off the ground,

Students in the proper setup for a hip ride. The side body surfaces should be in direct contact for a smooth transfer of weight.

At the peak of the lateral hip ride, shared weight centers are suspended over the plumb line of the supportive partner's base of support.

it is important for partner B to simply undercurve and then lean directly into partner A. In this moment, a common instinct is for the lifted partner to jump to lift themselves up onto partner A; however, jumping disconnects the zippered side–body connection and moves their weight up instead of laterally over the base of their partner where it is needed. Partner B can help immensely in this action by maintaining the side–body connection and pressing down firmly with their left arm across the shoulders of their lifting partner. This will add leverage, help the partners stay connected, and make them feel lighter. Have students switch roles and practice both sides, reflecting all instructions.

## ROCKING HORSE

The rocking horse, or sagittal hip ride, is similar to a lateral hip ride, except the partner orientation and the direction of undercurve and weight shift differ. In the rocking horse, supportive partner A begins by facing the back of partner B in a lunge with the working, shelving leg forward between the legs of standing partner B. With their right leg forward and left leg back in a stable lunge, partner A wraps their right arm around partner B's waist, draws their bodies close together (like the lateral side–body zipper effect), and places their left hand broadly on partner B's left side. With their weight forward onto their right leg, partner A executes a moderately rotated fourth position undercurve to their back (left) leg and takes their partner's weight back onto their front, with partner B sitting on the raised shelf of partner A's right thigh. With partner A's head aligned to the left of partner B's head, partner B can effectively press back into partner A and lean their head back as in a reclined armchair. Just as in the lateral hip ride, it is vital that partner B does not jump but moves back with their partner, allowing their partner to leverage their weight up while maintaining the connection between their bodies. At the top of the action, partner A will lengthen the standing back leg to suspend both of their weight centers for a moment before rocking back down, making sure to plié on the standing leg as they fall back toward standing and then moving back through the same undercurve motion used to enter the lift.

At the peak of a rocking horse sagittal hip ride, shared weight centers are suspended over the plumb line of the supportive partner.

> continued

### Modifications and Problem-Solving

The most common issues students encounter are disconnections between weight centers, an impulse to jump when being lifted, and lifting partners not shifting their weight (and that of their partner) far enough up and over the standing leg. Fear is a factor, so building up to full suspension over the plumb line is helpful for partners to calibrate how much weight shift and thrust is required for suspension. To troubleshoot generally, the instructor should observe students' attempts and locate which issues are at play. Check the use of undercurve, strength in the legs, maintenance of torso connection, and direction of weight shift rather than using a jumping action.

### Expanding and Advanced Skills

There are many variations of hip ride mechanics. With advanced or practiced students, open workshopping of creative adaptations can offer exciting opportunities for exploration and help build confidence as they discover unique versions of the lifting action.

Redirections are common variations worth exploring. Build the range by coaching students toward exploring a one-quarter and one-half redirection at the top of the hip ride, moving their partner through space, and adding a bit of momentum. For a lateral hip ride to the left, partner A turns out their standing leg and rotates counterclockwise one-quarter rotation, feeling the ease of balance at the crest of the plumb line before rotating the top of their standing leg inward and coming down 90 degrees to the left. To rotate open or clockwise (in this iteration), partner A begins with a parallel left standing leg and rotates the top of the leg out using their standing leg's turnout range to move 90 degrees to their right. To execute a one-half or 180-degree rotation, the supportive partner must suspend at the peak of the ride for slightly longer and turn the heel of their standing leg toward the rotation of redirection. See the video examples for more advanced variations and a visual breakdown of the mechanics described here. Another option is for students to maintain their bodily connection and arm grip but rock from one partner to the other, passing through a shared undercurve action. Students often smile and laugh at the joyful flight achieved in this back-and-forth action and become more confident as supportive partners.

▶ HIP RIDES: ADVANCED VARIATIONS

More advanced variations, mobilizing the action through space.

# PROMENADE

## Background

The term *promenade* means to stroll. For the purposes of this book, promenades are an exploration in which the revolution of one partner results from the strolling pathway of the other partner. Approaching promenades like a balance allows the supportive partner to act as a guide and a source of rotation or mobility. Students may find it exhilarating to be completely stable and have someone rotate them. Promenades are a great example of how an effective connection between partners can produce efficiency. Because promenades occur in a circular motion and require attention to friction (not to mention understanding and maintenance of a solid frame of the body), they are an excellent fundamental exercise to explore when creating and choreographing partnering. The seamless revolution of a dancer, common in both classical and contemporary dance, is beautiful to watch. Just as classical ballet maintains a plumb line within the form, contemporary styles often integrate off-center axes within promenades. In more advanced sequences, promenades can be paired with other partnered explorations to transition momentum and energy into or out of the rotational motion.

## Purpose

Partnered promenades explore the ease of circular revolution through a support or framework and can lead to exciting forms of momentum, speed, and efficiency. One dancer creates the motion of the promenade and thus must ensure that the other dancer is on their leg at all times, turning around a central axis. Both dancers must hold their shape or posture and agreed-upon relational alignment to execute the promenade as smoothly as possible. Promenades become a useful tool in the overall study of weight, balance, and circular force, while providing insight into the subtlety and nuance of effort.

Students demonstrate a promenade supportive position, with a hand-to-hand connection, facing each other.

### Foundational Exercises

#### SETTING UP

Dancers can explore the importance of stability in a balanced position in preparation for promenades. In other words, promenades rely on having a supportive partner to facilitate the supported partner's rotation around the vertical plumb line. It is imperative, however, that the supported partner has a clear sense of center and the ability to locate their own weight center. A passé balance, for example, shows that dancers are familiar with placing their weight over one foot with level hips. Dancers can explore movement individually when their shoulders and hips rotate as one unit at the barre or while holding onto the wall. For both dancers, there is an emphasis on the feet being strong and articulate whether they are walking or pivoting. The typical method of turning the heel repeatedly during solo promenades, as in ballet adagio material, is less related to partnered promenades because the maintenance of a strong supportive standing leg is vital, along with an active relevé on the foot, which lessens friction due to less surface area of the foot connecting with the floor. The most extreme example of this dynamic is the use of the pointe shoe, because it has a small surface area and its satin fabric allows for even less friction. In contemporary partnering and other forms, a similar condition can be achieved with the use of ballet slippers, jazz shoes, or socks.

### ▶ BALLET PROMENADE

Ballet promenades are demonstrated.

#### WORKSHOPPING

Promenades rely on a strong foundational sense of shared support. Although strong and stable body integration is required, there is a suppleness and ease that, when located, allows for small adjustments and a more synergistic connection between partners. Have dancers locate this engagement on their own before working with a partner. As done in the balance at the end of a barre exercise in ballet class, use the barres on the wall or a stationary barre to practice the soft stability of the upper body while activating a high, engaged relevé on the supporting side.

As explained in chapter 3, isometric muscle engagement involves activating a muscle without changing its length. Isometric activation is needed for both the supportive and supported partner in a promenade action. By exploring isometric connections within their own structure, students can integrate a sense of connection between the upper and lower body. Likewise, similar to how students might increase their own sense of resistance within a high plank by pushing away from the ground, similar explorations of resistance can serve as preparation for promenades. For dancers studying classical promenades en pointe, trying promenades at the ballet barre can also help them feel the revolution through the foot's spiral energy into the ground and tune up the strength and activation of the feet and legs.

### In Practice: Promenade

Objective: To explore the rotation of a dancer supported through the circular locomotion of another.

#### HAND-TO-WAIST PROMENADE

Partner A stands directly behind partner B with their hands on partner B's hips just below the natural waist. Partner B lifts their leg into a position that they can hold, such as passé, coupé, or front attitude. Partner A locates partner B's center of weight along the vertical plumb line and begins to revolve, walking in an even circle around partner B. Just like a pirouette can revolve en dehors (outward) or en dedans (inward), the promenade can rotate toward the direction of the working leg or toward the supporting leg. The supportive partner should angle diagonally toward the direction of rotation in the lower body and maintain the upper body as square to their partner as possible. With the upper body square, a frame (like in a ballroom dance closed position) can be established and maintained. The angle of the lower body allows a clearer step pattern with the feet moving forward while maintaining a stable distance from the supported partner. If the partner's lower body is also square and facing in, then they must cross the trailing leg over the leading leg or, worse, shuffle their feet open and closed sideways around the circle. Using a stable twist in the mid-body allows for this slight rotation of alignment between the upper and lower body, relative to the partner they are supporting.

## HAND TO HAND: FACING

Partners A and B directly face one another with their arms stretched out into second position or as if they are about to make a perpendicular frame to the floor. The supporting partner should offer broad, open palms with the fingers to the sides and the thumbs upward. The supported partner can then grasp their partner's hands in the space between the thumbs and forefingers, as they would hold onto the barre when facing it directly. With the elbows

The supportive partner demonstrates a promenade of their supported partner with a hand-to-waist connection in attitude devant.

lifted and supported but still slightly pliable, the dancers press into one another, establishing the frame and stable connection. Partner B lifts one leg. Immediately, partner A should sense any change in weight and move partner B's center of gravity over the standing leg and along the vertical plumb line. As referenced in the previous workshopping section, both partners sense the plumb line as the placement of most ease. Beyond the strength in the leg and foot and stability in the arms, gravity will be directly in line and the weighted feeling of falling will be minimized if the weight center is over the base of support along the plumb line. Using this stabilized frame and solid connection, partner A walks in a circle and both partners work to maintain their shoulders square to one another. The supportive partner (partner A) should angle their lower body to walk in the direction of rotation as noted earlier.

## ONE-HANDED PROMENADE

In this more advanced expression of an on-center ballet-style promenade, a one-handed connection between partners is used. Partners A and B link through a grasp or clasp like a handshake. A contralateral (cross-body) grip is the most stable, with both partners joining either their right or left hands. The frame created between their working shoulders aims to maintain a square relationship, but the arms create an S shape within the square as the point of contact. The elbows should remain lifted and supported from underneath the arms, but supple ease in the elbow joints is important for negotiating the small shifts and twists that might occur. The supportive partner (partner A) also presses up, creating a stable connection (like a ballet barre); in contrast, the supported partner (partner B) should press down slightly. The up-down action counters push through the hands, and the maintenance of the square frame allows a stable

> *continued*

Partners demonstrate a handshake or contralateral promenade connecting with one-handed support.

connection between partners that is then rotated with the walking action of the supporting partner (partner A) around the supported partner (partner B). This pivot can happen on the ball of the foot or another surface area. Success in this more open-frame connection demands ease within stability for the balance and relationship to be maintained.

## Modifications and Problem-Solving

Promenades might look easy, but looks can be deceiving. There are several key components to seamless promenades, including activation of a supple but stable frame and a sensitive connection between partners. When the shoulders and hips rotate as one unit, integrating the upper and lower body, the transfer of energy from the shared connection to the frame of the dancer being promenaded is more efficient. Promenades become the ultimate interplay between resistance in one's own body and in conversation with the connection and torque from a partner.

Common challenges in effective promenade actions are the breakdown of a clear pathway, uneven resistance or support, an uneven rate of rotation, and the collapse of a balanced upper body connection between partners. For the supportive partner, performing an even rotation around a fixed point is vital for upright, formal promenades. It is equally important for the supportive partner to maintain an equal distance from the supported partner as they move around them. Often, students in the supportive role walk into the imaginary zone of equidistance around the supported partner. I encourage students to imagine a ditch or a moat with water surrounding the central point of rotation, and I reinforce that they should not cross into that zone or else balance along the vertical axis (plumb line) is interrupted. Another common mistake is the shuffle action that dancers often fall into when first learning promenades. To directly face their supported partner, the supportive partner often steps sideways along the circular path and then brings the trailing leg to join it. This square alignment toward the center point, and the shuffle action of the feet, inhibits a smooth and even rate of rotation. To correct this, have the supportive partner practice turning their pelvis at an angle away from the supported partner, toward the direction of travel. This frame will also require cross-body stability in the support of the upper body but allows for a smoother walking action around the circle.

Challenges with maintenance of the upper body frame are also common in the practice of promenades. An assertive, forceful action from the supported partner is often the motion that collapses the frame and causes disconnection between partners. For dancers being supported in this way, it is often instinct to push off of a partner, like at the barre, and effectively try to rotate. This action essentially robs the supportive partner of the possibility of a smooth, even supportive action. Although students should be encouraged to be patient and allow the supportive partner to initiate the rotation, the supported partner is not passive. The malleability of the elbow joint, in particular, allows for minor adjustments, and the isometric muscle engagement creating resistance allows the supported partner to assist in the rotating action of promenade.

## Expanding and Advanced Skills

Promenades can occur with movement developments and embellishments. During a promenade, a dancer can développé the working leg or initiate several body parts as they revolve. During the revolution, the supportive partner can switch the connection with their partner, leaving the viewer with exciting moments of the supported partner being without support for a magical moment. Speed and rate of rotation also are effective when practiced at a more advanced level. Working on interesting transitions into and out of the promenade can also aid in the practice of more complexity. When can a promenade seemingly come out of nowhere? How might it evolve when the supported dancer is moving within the rotation rather than holding a stable shape? Reducing the points of connection and support also complicates the exploration with a higher level of difficulty.

EXERCISE 15
## EXERCISE 15
# TRADITIONAL LIFTS

### Background

Partnering with an emphasis on lifts can add excitement to a piece. Lifts can be the aspects of a dance that embody a peak or climax in the music or bring together a group of dancers in the apex of a work. Like many partnered explorations, traditional lifts require acute awareness of timing, weight distribution, and harnessing of upward momentum and leverage. Proper, efficient mechanics are also vital for safe expressions of lifts. Partners learn to negotiate weight with the preciseness and buoyancy that often result in lifts that seem effortless. Within traditional lifts, dancers are often performing opposite tasks. While one dancer is being launched into the air by igniting their use of a plié and jump and perhaps holding their frame in a taut manner on the perch of another dancer, their partner is rooted into the ground and negotiating their own sense of balance and support. When a group of dancers come together when timing is especially essential because more than one person is lifting a dancer, the group lifting must coordinate and work as a solid unit.

### Purpose

Traditional lifts are impressive. In choreography or classroom exploration, there are times when a dancer must turn all of their body weight over to their partner. As in solo work, some steps cannot be executed without commitment and sound mechanics. Traditional lifts call on the athleticism of both parties, and upper body and back strength often is imperative for lifting and serving as a counterweight when being lifted. By building strength over time, the movement potential becomes more versatile and the pictures that a dancer can create with their partner multiply. The simplest mechanics for traditional lifts still apply to the most advanced explorations. This approach is one of the most common when dancers think about partnering, but it also serves as the factor that discourages many from trying it. Strength is certainly required in many traditional lifts. Yet if a dancer can locate and use momentum from the lifted partner's effort and leverage their own upper and lower body away from the floor, they are capable of more than they can imagine.

### Foundational Exercises

#### WORKSHOPPING

In workshopping traditional lifts, remind students that floorwork and the ability to stack the body is key to many technical training ideals and processes. Lifting, pressing, and traveling with a partner in an improvisational setting can be a great way to problem-solve within these fundamental connections. Once a basic understanding of technique and safe mechanics is established, more freedom of exploration through improvisation allows both dancers to develop a more responsive and intuitive approach to lifting.

When attempting or planning a new lift, take time to map out the entry and landing footwork for both partners in advance. Have students practice the lift on a lower, smaller scale to learn the pattern of takeoff and descent. They can then work up to a higher, fuller expression of the lift. Although higher press lifts are often only truly possible in their full range with the arms strong and locked, it is beneficial to map out the beginning and end of the lift's action without the pressure of executing the full lift right away.

### In Practice: Traditional Lifts

Objective: To explore the power and kinetics of lifting and being supported.

Several simplified exercises lead to a successful practice of traditional lifts. Partners in dance company rehearsal settings often seem to find ease within these physically demanding exercises and steps. A closer look reveals that partners work to synchronize their timing, impulses, and initial connections. An in-depth examination of lifts or troubleshooting lifting techniques might mean looking at several key introductory exercises, including assisted jumps with a careful descent, press lifts with a stable connection or initiation, or traveling jumps with clear follow-through and a continuation of the connection between partners.

## ASSISTED JUMPS (IN PLACE)

In partnering class and even in establishing connections within a rehearsal, practicing assisted sautés or other leaps are a great place to start. There are a plethora of iterations for assisting another dancer with a jump. For the purposes of fundamental lifting, this exercise looks at a typical connection found within classical and contemporary dance contexts. With one dancer behind another and both dancers facing forward, the upstage dancer places their hands on their partner's waist. Hand placement is vital, and communication is key. Working with a partner to feel what is comfortable and specific to that person's structure is also essential when it comes to the sensitive areas of the abdominal cavity and torso.

Specifically, with an assisted jump in place, there should be a dispersed connection inward and then upward within the hands, without the fingernails digging into the dancer within the lift. I use the image of an oven mitt to help students think of the cup or the whole hand with long fingertips, rather than individual fingers pinching inward. The thumb is the most likely to dig in; depending on the lift, the thumb can be tucked along the same direction as the other fingers.

Students demonstrate as assisted jump (in place), viewed on an angle.

## ▶ TRADITIONAL LIFTS FROM BALLET PARTNERING: PART I

**Dancers demonstrate assisted jumps in place.**

The dancer to be lifted takes a plié, and their lifting partner mimics their plié and assists with their jump. Timing is everything. Dancers must synchronize, and the hand-to-waist connection acts as energy toward furthering the jump upward, and then also as resistance supporting the descent and landing. For maximum efficiency, advise the lifting partner to try and activate their upward effort just before the apex of the lifted partner's jump. Why double up the effort? That sensitivity and efficiency then allows the lifting partner to further the extent of their partner's jump while reserving energy and strength for a safe, resistive descent in the jump's landing. Proximity is also key within assisted jumps in place. The supportive dancer must be cautious that their chin or face is not in the path of their partner's shoulders. The dropping of the pelvis underneath the upper portion of the body (for both partners) ensures an obstacle-free upward trajectory.

## PRESS LIFT

One of the most exhilarating feelings is when students feel the physics of dance through the successful application of thrust, leverage, and use of momentum. This is how dancers seem to defy gravity. When an assisted jump turns into a full press lift with arms fully extended and stacked to achieve a lift, there is a *wow moment*. The mechanics of pressing, like assisted jumps, is not based on strength alone but also on the combination of kinetic power and timing. Avoiding the sensation of locking out the arms is important for safety and allows for reflexive activation during the lift and when entering and exiting from them. A locked joint can be dangerous, whereas an extended joint with proper alignment can be a great way to create ease

> *continued*

within a lift. Technically, aim to stack the arms over the supportive bases of the shoulders or hip girdles. Aligning a lifted partner's weight center over that same base of support allows for a greater sense of ease for both partners. Pressing or lifting is experienced in everyday life, such as reach for an item on the highest shelf or carrying furniture overhead. Framing these actions as rooted in day-to-day motions might help students reluctant to attempt assisted jumps or press lifts.

## TRAVELING JUMPS

Traveling jumps often build on assisted jumps and pressing but add the challenge of locomoting with a partner. Dancers must travel together with an awareness of where their partner is in space. In an across-the-floor sequence in ballet class such as a tombé, pas de bourrée, or pas de chat, the dancer jumping will have force and momentum propelling them forward. The supportive partner must access the waist-to-hand connection and be ready to morph that momentum upward into a lift or press. A common tendency in traveling lift passages is for the supportive, lifting partner to trail behind the momentum of the supported partner. Rather than trail behind, the supportive partner should be leading, relative to the direction of travel, and then essentially pass their partner across their own body in the traveling jump. This setup allows the lifting partner to arrest forward momentum while activating the lift by planting, using the power in the lower body, and lining up the highest point of the lift over their own base of support. When trailing behind, dancers only have their arm strength to rely on to lift, and even that power is ineffective as their partner is effectively jumping away from them.

Students demonstrate the peak of a supported pas de chat, viewed from the side.

▶ **TRADITIONAL LIFTS FROM BALLET PARTNERING: PART II**

Dancers demonstrate basic traveling pas de chat lift.

## Modifications and Problem-Solving

Traditional lifts call for complete trust and full commitment. It can be disorienting to jump as high as possible while being supported. By reminding students about the basics of touch, safe engagement of the 360-degree core, and efficient use of the lower body's power, traditional lifts can be accomplished and can be fun. As in many other exercises, communication is key to a fruitful exploration of traditional lifts. By keeping an open dialogue between partners and even with the instructor or another outside eye, the technique and mechanics of a lift can be the focus and allow students to not take feedback of what to adjust or change personally.

When approaching a new partnership, it can be helpful for the lifting partner to observe the partner they will lift, jumping alone in the manner of the lift that will be executed. This allows the lifting partner to locate the approximate apex of a partner's jump and zoom out to familiarize themselves with the rhythm and pattern of a partner's preparation and takeoff action.

Another common issue that can arise in the more formal, upright assisted lifts and presses is the instinctual tendency of the dancer being lifted to throw their head backward and almost jump back and into their supportive partner. Instinct might kick in as if this action were helpful, but it often simply becomes a safety hazard for the lifting partner's face and head. Instead, the lifted dancer should imagine that they are doing the jump on their own and try to maintain a vertical trajectory. If the lifted partner maintains a sense of uprightness, then the lifted partner can step forward directly under the weight center if the lift is in the pressed range above the supportive partner's shoulders. If an upper back arch to offer a shelf is used, the lifted partner should engage that shape once they are lifted above their supportive partner's head line. The action of arching up and back, above the support of their partner, then becomes seamless and synergistic with the forward step of the lifting partner. Coordination, timing, and communication all come into play when troubleshooting traditional lifts.

## Expanding and Advanced Skills

To gear up for ways to expand an exercise or skill, three distinct approaches that can help elaborate on traditional lifts: timing or speed, direction, and quality. A press lift can soar quickly, or a shelf press can make two revolutions. Dancers may find that by adding a revolution or by changing the timing of the lift, the lift itself is completely altered and reinvented. As expressed in the earlier sections on choreography, finding unique and seamless transitions into and out of lifts is essential if the aim is to use partnering authentically in a dance. By weaving lifts and partnered material into the full material of the dance, the instructor can smooth out the often jolting, disjointed activation of partnering when an integrated approach is less emphasized by a choreographer.

Students demonstrate a press.

Another layer that contributes to the wow factor in a press is that the dancer being supported provides a shelf or surface for the supportive partner to access and press against. For the purposes of this book, look at the lifted dancer in a back extension with arms up in line with the crown of the head. In this case, the shelf becomes the upper back and, again, the point of connection is with hands open, connecting to the broad plane of the back of the shoulder and underneath the scapula bones.

## ▶ TRADITIONAL LIFTS FROM BALLET PARTNERING: PART III

Dancers demonstrate a long, sustained traveling lift using a scapular shelf and carrying approach (advanced skill), and arabesque variation with same mechanics.

Timing is key when pressing is taught. A familiar model for safe lifting action is competitive weightlifting. The clean and jerk action in weightlifting is similar to that of press lifts. Although it might seem counterintuitive for a student working on lifting technique, the first action is to drop their weight down in a plié or parallel fourth position as the supported partner jumps. By lowering the base of support, the power of the legs can be fully engaged and the arms can extend while the partner is still moving upward in the power of their own jump. Once the bend of the lower body and extension of the upper body is achieved, the lifting partner can maintain a stable upper body while extending their legs to stand and moving the lifted partner up. This all happens in just a moment, so it is important to practice and get the physical pattern of the leg action to execute the lift within the timing of a partner's jump.

## EXERCISE 16
# INITIATION AND SUGGESTION

### Background

Initiation and suggestion is a widely used form of non-weight-bearing partnering. In more forceful (and perhaps negative) variations, it might be referred to as *manipulation*. The difference is specifically related to the intent, amount of force, and sensitivity employed within a similar technique. Whereas manipulation tends to inhibit agency and choice for the more passive partner with a puppet-like expression, a more nuanced and reflexive approach to this principle is *initiation* or *suggestion*. With varied degrees of touch using a range of force, directional suggestion, and external action on a partner's body, this version increases decision making and responsiveness from the partner receiving touch. Like an external stimulus or catalyst, the active partner's connection to the receptive partner can range from a simple indication of which limb or body zone to move or a weighted connection that directs the action of their partner and sends them locomoting into space. Once trust and reflexive nonverbal communication are established, dancers can overlap initiation and suggestion to incite and inspire more complex movement sequences. Taking it a step further, a duo, trio, or small group may explore the principle with all dancers functioning as both initiators and receivers of touch and suggestion. With a truly balanced effort and power dynamic in this format, the partnership or group connection expresses a deep engagement and investment between partners rather than a sense of domination or manipulation. This exercise requires relationship building and patience. Initiation and suggestion involves witnessing the response of another person when an individual nonverbally suggests where to go or what to do.

### ▶ INITIATION AND SUGGESTION IMPROVISATION

Part I: Two dancers explore a small version of the exercise by mutually initiating and sensing the movement suggestions of their partner via touch through the hands. Use of whole palm, fingertips, and the back of the hand serve as a good warm-up to the full exploration of the exercise to come.

Part II: Two dancers explore initiation and suggestion, with one partner initiating and one responding.

Part III: Two dancers explore initiation and suggestion by overlapping the two roles of input and responsiveness.

Part IV: A trio of dancers demonstrate a version with two initiators giving input to one partner receiving and responding.

### Purpose

In life, as in dance, a connection must begin somewhere and often originates in a moment of noticing. Initiation and suggestion can develop sensitive, responsive attention to one's partner. Teachers must prepare students for the dynamics of trust and open-mindedness when giving and receiving touch in this manner. As an exercise with a lower amount of weight-bearing, the risk level is lower, but the yield is great in its effectiveness in honing nonverbal communication skills within partnering. Initiation and suggestion are closely related to the dynamics of leading and following in social dance and ballroom forms, and these skills can be developed over time and deepened within an ongoing partnership to foster a seamlessness and organic connection between dancers.

### Foundational Exercises

Foundational exercises for initiation and suggestion can build on many of the exercises discussed in chapters 2 (exercise 2, Trust Building; and exercise 3, Active and Passive) and 3 (exercise 9, Redirection and Leverage). The common thread within these foundational exercises is their development of attention to internal energy and choice making within the partnership. By tuning into one another, a meaningful and functional connection between dancers occurs.

## GRASP AND CLASP

Exercise 1, Grasp and Clasp, is a great warm-up for exercise 16 because it is rooted in reconnection with nuanced degrees of touch through the hands with minimal weight sharing.

## PALM TO PALM

Take exercise 1 further by leading students in a tai chi–inspired exploration of degrees of touch. Have students take a wide stance, soften their knees, and place their palms against their partner's palms. By giving and receiving touch and pushing between the partners, pressure can increase, which requires yielding by the receptive partner to also increase. By aligning the give and take of pressure and touch, the pair might even locomote through space. Maintaining a soft, malleable lower body allows students to follow the direction and flow with their partner with ease and possibility. Once students become comfortable with more drive, pressure, and momentum in this warm-up exploration, zoom out to a lighter connection with a lower degree of weight and pressure to determine whether the connection and direction are as easy for students to read and respond to.

## In Practice: Initiation and Suggestion

Objective: To explore nonverbal communication through touch and to develop sensitivity and nuance in a range of degrees of touch, suggestion, and follow-through, while learning to receive touch and respond to touch-based input from a partner.

## LIGHT TOUCH OR TAP AND MOVE

To begin an exploration of initiation and suggestion, one partner uses a light touch with an open hand or other body part to signal a part of the body or zone to activate in the receptive partner. This simple version of the exercise can allow students to become comfortable with one another, get used to touch in a direct manner, and hone physical listening skills before using a more weighted connection.

Designate one partner as the receptive partner (partner A) and the other as the initiator (partner B). Begin with subtle initiations to specific parts of the body. Examples include a light touch on the back of the right knee, a gentle nudge of the left shoulder or back of the head, a soft brush of one foot on the calf of the receptive partner, or the back of the forearm connecting with the lower spine. With these isolated initiation points and movement suggestions, allow time for each signal to be received and activated before adding another. For the active partner, observation of the pathways and outcomes can be fruitful for student understanding that a receptive partner will most often not move in the way or manner one might expect in response to a particular initiation. Allowing space and time for a receptive partner to resolve a given initiation allows the active, initiating partner to tune into physical listening.

It is helpful for the receptive partner to close their eyes to tune into the initiating partner's touch and work to respond authentically in turn. When their eyes are open and individuals see themselves in the mirror, prejudgment, anticipatory planning, and less authentic responses often occur. Closed eyes certainly require trust and adequate space between duos exploring the exercise, but even a heavy-lidded, soft focus of the eyes will allow the receptive partner to feel a more internal sensation.

## CONNECT AND FOLLOW-THROUGH

To deepen the connection between partners or increase the movement outcomes of this improvised exploration of suggestion through touch, begin to increase the range of the initiations and follow-through to signal a direction to travel in space. As the range increases, the amount of weight in a connection increases as well. In particular, initiation of the lower body might include a directional weight transfer to allow for mobility. Still avoiding a full grip on a partner's limbs, use a strong open palm or the back of the hand to connect, take a bit of weight, and direct a partner into space. With a more sustained connection and directional suggestion, the dance can

> continued

become less linear and truncated and dancers begin to find three-dimensional, circular flow in the movement.

## ▶ CONNECT AND FOLLOW-THROUGH

Partner A uses connection to direct partner B in space. Partners switch roles.

Provide this helpful tip to the receptive partner: give a bit of effort to creating a resistive energy at the points of contact. This is not to say that the receptive partner should be rigid or unmoving; rather, pushing back slightly into their partner allows them to maintain the point of connection, provides longer directional suggestions, and signals the amount of weight used in a movement to the initiating partner.

### Modifications and Problem-Solving

Initiation and suggestion can be difficult for some students, relative to sensing and authentically responding to a given touch, gesture, or guided action. Many students receive the input but then execute movement that is unrelated to their partner's physical suggestion or initiation. Encourage students to slow down and respond only with the degree of movement related to the degree of touch and pressure, the duration of the connected action, and the trajectory of the follow-through. Only by working to achieve authentic responses will the initiating partner begin to understand how a particular touch or gesture manifests in their partner's movement.

Closed eyes are helpful because they allow for small, subtle responses at first and then build toward more complex, large-scale, and layered movement. This might occur within a few rounds of the exploration, over the course of a whole class, or even over practice of the exercise over multiple class meetings. The payoff is worth the wait, and initiation and suggestion can be helpful in developing sensitivity, responsiveness, and nonverbal communication.

Challenges might arise, however, with regard to the effectiveness of an active partner's touch or discomfort from indirect or insensitive touch. It might seem silly, but the Golden Rule (treat others how you would like to be treated) is an effective frame for the use of intentional, respectful touch and initiation. It can be particularly helpful for younger, less mature students who may use silliness as a response to discomfort.

When the instructor is working with a less experienced or less familiar group of dancers, it might also be helpful to take a moment to agree on safe, comfortable zones of the body before beginning with a new partner. Each student will likely have differing degrees of comfort and openness to touch, so clear communication and boundary setting can be helpful even if only to allow students to understand the vital need for respectful touch. One helpful tool is the red, yellow, and green check-in. Individuals use their own hands to identify zones of the body that are red (no touch), yellow (moderate touch only if necessary), or green (open to touch). Use this exercise at the start of each class to engage the whole group or in one-on-one settings when selecting or assigning partners for the first time that class.

### Expanding and Advanced Skills

As explained earlier in the discussion on connection and follow-through, natural progressions toward more advanced explorations of exercise 16 will emerge through multiple rounds of switching roles, discussions of the dynamics and outcomes between rounds, and with the comfort that emerges quickly through practice. Common expansions of the level of difficulty will emerge when speed is increased, when initiations from the active partner are overlapped for more complexity, or if a receptive partner receives movement suggestions from more than one partner. When practicing in trios or small groups, it is even more important to listen and exercise patience so as not to overwhelm the partner receiving initiations. Another way to add complexity is by having a pair of dancers both act as receivers and initiators in a reflexive mode. Each dancer can shift between roles organically over time, or they can develop their perceptiveness and reading of motion and then respond to what they notice as opportunities for initiation of their partner while continuing to listen and respond to their partner's touch in turn.

## EXERCISE 17
# ROLLING POINTS

### Background

The rolling points exercise and partnered exploration is easily mistaken for contact improvisation. Although it shares many similarities with the connection and mobilization in contact improvisation, this application is drawn from a partnered technique I learned while dancing in the company, Shen Wei Dance Arts. Featured prominently in Shen Wei's piece *Connect Transfer* (Wei 2004), the shared point or points of connection are mobilized through a circular, rotational action in the body that allows for fluid and unexpected outcomes within duet or group interactions. During the latter half of the piece, rolling points are activated within a series of stunning duets using circular momentum and flow. Later, rolling points are activated in a five-dancer sequence referred to informally within the company as the Jackson 5, in which all dancers remain connected as they spill, dive, revolve, and locomote across the stage. The group expression of rolling points is also featured in the opening sequence of Shen Wei's *Re-Part II* (Wei 2007), which uses the concept within a full 12-dancer lineup with all dancers connected and flowing together.

### Purpose

Rolling points is a challenging but exciting exercise for more advanced partnering students. Although it can certainly be explored and practiced among beginning dancers, the full, momentum-driven version of this exercise is well suited as a challenge for experienced dancers. This exercise calls on the dancer to give in to the drive and flow of a shared trajectory with a partner, using a subtle weight-sharing action to maintain a connection while continuously moving through space. A challenge for students that comes when fully engaged in the exercise is the inability to think or plan, but rather the necessity of nuanced physical listening, and yielding to one's partner and to the movement principle itself.

### Foundational Exercises

#### PREPARING THE BODY

To allow for full access to all body surfaces and increase the range of potential points of contact, dancers must warm up the head, neck, torso, and hips in particular. Students start in the cat yoga position while on their hands and knees, and then they move through the cow position. Next, they activate lateral flexion side to side, maintaining the torso parallel to the floor. They connect those actions by circling the torso in both directions, moving through cat, cow, and lateral flexion and keeping the head and tail moving together. Use any other stretch, warm-up, or activation exercise that will help students not only prepare for a safe exploration of rolling points but also expand the potential points of connection their body can access.

#### WORKSHOPPING

Although the true application of rolling points engages two or more dancers in contact, solo dancers can explore the round shape of the body, continuously shining away from the point of contact with the wall, mirror, or floor. Shining away refers to the parts of the body that are not in direct contact with a partner or supportive surface reaching in the opposite direction, effectively lessening their full weight. Like many of the setups for other exercises offered in this book, removing the pressure of working with a partner immediately is a safe and effective way for dancers to become comfortable with the concept and the technique required.

▶ ROLLING POINTS: SOLO EXPLORATION

Solo dancers explore the point of contact with a mirrored wall and then supporting a Yoga ball against the mirrored wall.

> *continued*

Take space on a stable flat surface, and have dancers begin exploring their own connection through a single point. By following the flow of movement and accessing their weight through subtle off-center movement, they can begin to locate the circular flow of the action while remaining connected to their supportive surface. Consider these questions: How does a point of contact with the back of the hand roll and flow down the outside of the forearm, laterally across rounded shoulder blades in the upper back, and down the other arm? Can students explore a round rolling surface of the front of the arms and across the sternum? This action requires a broad, open curve of the front of the body, reaching into the backspace. What does it feel like to change one's axis and send the point of contact rolling diagonally down and across the back, connecting with the outside of one hip and allowing the surfaces of the pelvis and lumbar spine to connect and flow?

Solo dancers practice the proper positioning of the body using the support of a flat, vertical surface.

## In Practice: Rolling Points

Objective: To develop a fluid connection to another dancer and allow oneself to yield to the momentum and trajectory of connected circular pathways.

### ROLLING POINTS VIA IMPROVISATION

Improvisation is one of the best ways for students to become familiar with the mechanics of the rolling points exercise and work within a speed and range that feels comfortable to both partners. Have dancers find a partner and begin to work together as they did with their innate supportive surface when exploring on their own. Beginning back to back and rounding away from one another, dancers should start exploring the rock and flow by following a single shared point with the circular trajectory of rolling. It is important to keep suppleness and malleability in the feet, ankles, knees, and hips to allow the lower body to move, shift, and travel to maintain the point of connection while following the flow. As the dancers become more comfortable, encourage them to explore a greater range and more surfaces of the body. Incorporate pathways that connect and flow through the lower body and in three-dimensional pathways using diagonal shifts in the axis of one or both partners. If space allows, dancers might close or soften the focus of their eyes to shift their attention to internal sensation. As in prior exercises, the use or minimization of *seeing* helps dancers tap more substantially into *feeling*.

Partners demonstrate the optimal, round body shape for effective exploration of the rolling points concept.

### ▶ ROLLING POINTS: DUET IMPROVISATION

Dancers explore the rock and flow by following a single shared point with the circular trajectory of rolling.

### ROLLING POINTS IN SET MATERIAL

Although the exploration of this exercise is most authentically achieved through improvisation, setting a specific sequence of rolling points movement can allow students to study specific, expected pathways and connections and fine-tune the amount of weight, spill, flow, and follow-through required to fully execute the partnered phrase. Consider having each duet identify and demonstrate a successful connection and mobilization they found during improvisation, and connect them all to create a longer, known phrase. Or together with students, design a phrase with specific actions and directives and share information between pairs of students who found a successful execution of a given movement sequence.

## Modifications and Problem-Solving

Common dynamic challenges that will likely require troubleshooting in the practice of rolling points are disconnections and hiccups between partners' point of contact, rigid use of the legs that inhibits free flow and movement following the action of the movement, restricted torso flexibility, or discomfort connecting one's front body with another dancer. All of these

*> continued*

can be addressed independently. For the dynamics that cannot be adjusted (e.g., the range of a dancer's flexibility or mobility at the time), offer workarounds or encourage a focus on a different body zone.

Moving through different partnerships might also help students troubleshoot as they go. The successful approaches of one student can be shared with the next partner or the group. Challenging dynamics of uneven height, body type, or technical proficiency between partners can be worked around by simply accommodating each other's differences and adjusting one's approach as needed. For dancers who signal their discomfort (verbally or nonverbally) with close contact of the front of their body, encourage their partnership to thoroughly explore the back surfaces of the body and find creative pathways to route around sensitive areas of the body.

## Expanding and Advanced Skills

To activate a more challenging and advanced exploration of rolling points, encourage experienced partners to give in even more to the fall and spill of following momentum while maintaining weighted contact through the point of contact. The rate or speed of the action will naturally increase as students begin to yield their weight into gravity, effectively riding the wave of the movement. Closing the eyes aids dancers in finding internal sensation but also increases the challenge of the rolling points exercise when used within more vigorous explorations.

Like Shen Wei's Jackson 5 quintet in *Connect Transfer*, gradually increasing the number of dancers exploring rolling points at once also increases the level of difficulty and leads to even more unexpected outcomes. Within both approaches of the use of improvisational or set material, exploring in trios or quartets adds complexity and calls for more care, yielding, and physical listening among the group of partners.

## EXERCISE 18
# ME SCORE

### Background

Returning to the format of structured improvisation exercises or the use of improvised scores is a group-centered exploration called the Me score. Passed down by Bebe Miller (professor emerita, The Ohio State University) during her Partnered Improvisation course, the Me score uses a group dynamic with the focus of all students' attention and support going to one dancer at a time. Whoever calls out "Me!" becomes the focus of the whole group's awareness until another dancer calls out "Me!" in turn.

▶ ME SCORE

Group partnering improvisation.

### Purpose

The Me score draws on student willingness to take risks, develops individual assertiveness and clear physical communication, and requires students to be truly present, responsive, and in the moment, owing to the unpredictability of the exercise. In cross-training and physical therapy for high-performing dancers and athletes, the unpredictability of movement allows for the greatest strength building and motor function refinement. When the body learns repetitive pathways and familiar movements, it finds efficiency; new and unexpected action allows the body to respond and adapt. The Me score has this outcome but in the context of refined confidence and strength in partnering. The foundational skills and strength built up to that point are immediately called on as the student navigates the unknown actions of the Me role within their group. Likewise, the student learns how to become one of a few supporters where cooperative and coordinated support from several partners multiplies the potential outcome and excitement of a given lift or movement passage.

Note that warm-ups for this improvisational exploration should include workouts that engage the arms and stabilize the trunk by engaging the core muscles. Proper preparation of the body prevents potential strain attributable to the unpredictable nature of the score. See the Cross-Training and Preparatory Strengthening section in chapter 3 for warm-ups.

### Foundational Exercises

#### WORKSHOPPING

Practicing in a circle of trust is a great way to begin before conducting a full exploration of the Me score. In small groups of four to seven students, dancers make a small circle about arms-length apart. One dancer steps into the middle of the circle. This person will serve in the Me role, which will be explained more thoroughly later. Instruct the dancers in the center to plant their feet and soften their knees, creating a neutral base. The person in the center can then soften and fall in different, unexpected directions. The dancers in the circle take turns receiving the weight of the person in the middle with their hands (or other body parts to support), and then they return to their vertical plumb line before falling in another direction. This is a great time to reinforce maintaining a strong stable base with contralateral stability and keeping the pelvis upright with soft, responsive knees and an engaged core. Cycle through with each student taking a turn. To increase complexity, repeat the process while expanding the circle circumference, try it in smaller groups so dancers must cover a larger range of the imagined circle, or move into the more free-form exploration of the Me score.

Revisiting exercise 10, Over, Under, and Through, may also serve as a helpful warm-up and allow students to focus on each other in a one-on-one situation.

> continued

### In Practice: The Me Score

Objective: To foster group cooperation, awareness, and responsiveness within an improvisational partnering score, so students continue to gain confidence and assertive physical communication.

A group of students explores the Me score. Group partnering and the distribution of labor allow for even more dynamic lifts.

## EXPLORATION

For the Me score, it is good to begin with groups of four to six dancers, depending on the number of students. With larger groups, the space becomes crowded and causes some dancers to remain on the edges of the group. Practice with fewer dancers calls for much more strength, stamina, and awareness and can serve as an excellent step in expanding toward a more advanced exploration of the score.

In their small groups, dancers begin improvising in and around one another to explore the negative space while keeping tight proximity. Encourage students to tune into the energies and motion pathways of their whole group, sensing the location and trajectory of every other dancer. Once a group flow is established, any student in the group can call out "Me!" and their partners should then immediately respond by turning their attention and support toward that dancer. The Me role should take the lead by moving toward, into, through, and past their partners. Students then take support with direct, assertive choices and create opportunities for their group of partners to lift and further their movements by providing access to their limbs and weight center. When the timing feels right, any other dancer in the group can call out "Me!" and the attention should immediately shift to them (while making sure the previous Me is safely back in control of their own weight).

In this exploration, it is important for dancers to understand that they should not be passive and limp; rather, they should take responsibility for their own weight and participate as active partners even when being lifted and supported. When a partner finds an opportunity to support under a leg, arm, or torso, the Me person should push into that support for leverage, creating an engaged lightness. By keeping some degree of tone in all limbs and in the legs while standing upright, the Me individual will be ready and equipped to respond to movements initiated, redirected, or furthered by their group of partners. Likewise, the supportive students in the group should keep a malleable base with softness in their hips, knees, and ankles. Set up with a cross-stabilized stance and engaged core to be ready for movement in any direction. Supportive partners are then able to provide safe and reliable support without inadvertently hurting themselves in the process. The very unpredictability that characterizes the learning potential in this exercise can also lead to injury if students are not working mindfully.

## Modifications and Problem-Solving

### SPATIAL LIMITATION

Restrict the range and proximity of the group's members to a more contained space. This closeness allows the supported partner to feel more secure until trust within the group is built, and it provides a quicker opportunity for the supportive members in the group as they continue to hone and develop their awareness and responsiveness. This variation works best with groups of four to five dancers. With larger groups, the space becomes congested, which makes finding ways to be supportive even more challenging. As with most studio teaching, being aware of what students need and recognizing when to pause and clarify or reorganize groups is vital to fostering trust, confidence, and mindfulness within the class community. The listening that teachers encourage between student peers is also an integral aspect of teacher-to-student awareness. Keeping an improvisational mindset allows teachers to follow the flow and trajectory of a given class and models the very qualities and approach they are trying to communicate. Teachers can have a class plan and outline but still be ready to adapt and shift gears as the class energy dictates.

### MODERATION AND MODULATION

While beginning students acclimate to the Me score, an instructor might ask the Me to moderate the amount of weight they are giving partners as the group gets used to the experience.

> *continued*

Keeping their weight center closer to the plumb line over their base of support allows for more nuanced supportive responses as a place to begin. Limit the practice to low weight-bearing interactions where the individual in the Me role stays connected to the ground and does not yet develop into full weight lifting.

## Expanding and Advanced Skills

### FLOOR IS LAVA

To challenge more experienced dancers or to dig deeper, offer this prompt: the Me never touches the floor. Similar to the popular game, the Floor Is Lava, this application of the Me score presents a greater challenge because supportive partners must coordinate and cooperate even more to keep the Me dancer moving without needing to touch down in transition. Students can also be reminded that remaining off the floor does not only refer to overhead lifts. Previously learned skills like draping, shelving, and weight sharing can all come into play in this version of the exploration while maintaining the dancer aloft even at lower and mid-level heights.

### INDIVIDUAL SUPPORT

Restrict the score to call for only one-person support at any given moment. By requiring more of each individual to support the Me role on their own, this option requires more creative adaptation, listening, and supportive integrity. This iteration of the Me score is a solid example of an improvised partnering approach. Although it is related to contact improvisation, this approach calls for more delineation between the supportive and supported roles.

## SUMMARY

Chapter 4 ventured into the creative practices of dance and how they relate to potential when focused in dance partnering. The creative prompts and methods offered can serve as a springboard for the instructor's choreography and their students' work. Part III of the Practical Skills and Frameworks for Teaching Dance Partnering series introduced the most challenging and complex exercises in this book. See the ancillary materials and resources linked to chapter 4 in HK*Propel* for further examples and explanations of some of these techniques.

To conclude this book, chapter 5, Space: Fostering Community and Inclusive Pedagogy, focuses on the social, interpersonal, and community aspects unique to the dance partnering classroom. Teaching methods in support of a nongendered and inclusive approach are offered as a foundation of dynamics for instructors to consider and tailor to their educational platform and their community.

## DISCUSSION QUESTIONS

1. What role has improvisation played in your dancing career?

2. What creative methods and compositional techniques do you use in your own choreographic practice? How might those be turned into prompts for your students to explore and try out within a partnering context?

3. Thinking of the choreographers you have worked with, what approach did they take in the development of partnered material in their dances?

For additional information, see the ancillary materials and resources linked to this chapter in HK*Propel.*

UCSB students performing *Boys Like Us.*
Choreography by Brandon Whited.

© Fritz Olenberger

# 5

# SPACE: Fostering Community and Inclusive Pedagogy

## OVERVIEW

Educators must often make decisions about how to build community and create a bond of trust between students. As they delve into these considerations within the context of the dance partnering classroom, they find that many of the usual dynamics are heightened because of the intimate, somewhat risky, and often unfamiliar nature of partnering for many students. The dynamics of touch, consent, and individual agency are even more important in a place of vulnerability. Identity, self-assuredness, and mutual respect among the group are vital to the cultivation of trust and familiarity benefits deep exploration of dance partnering principles. This chapter explores creative frameworks and techniques for building classroom connectivity by answering questions like these: What type of class culture and space do educators want to foster and provide for their students? What toxic practices in training should be avoided or reframed to create a better environment for students? How can educators open the door for all students to feel safe, supported, and welcome? This chapter discusses creating a safe space and supportive environment and developing a community within the classroom and beyond.

### VOCABULARY

consent

inclusive pedagogy

student-centered pedagogy

subject-centered pedagogy

teacher-centered pedagogy

touch statement

For many educators, the principles of equity, diversity, inclusion, and access are vitally important to the class culture they want to facilitate. Yet for many, there is much work to do in these areas. Teacher awareness of these gaps and consideration of inclusive efforts is an important first step. Educators who came of age with a dedicated practice in dance may have had bad experiences previously, were exposed to negative frameworks, or endured toxic practices along the way. Within a formal study such as dance, tradition is often considered before student needs. Consequently, the practice itself becomes the most important element in the studio as opposed to the living student-artists the instructors are there to teach. Shifting the emphasis and lens of priority toward students in balance with the instructor's knowledge and expertise and the principles of the subject can deepen student engagement, increase pride and accomplishment, and improve growth.

This chapter considers practical and holistic approaches to creating a richly engaging and actively inviting class culture. By considering these ideas from a pedagogical stand-point, educators can foster trust, communication, connection, inclusion, and cooperation. Students are given the reins to develop their peer leadership skills and to demonstrate the collective power and potential of a group working together. Although the exercises offered in chapters 2 through 4 are mostly built on duet partnering, they can be modified to explore the techniques within small-group formats once students become familiar with the concepts in one-on-one practice. Learning to partner with more than one person allows for deeper development of sensitive physical listening and awareness, resulting from the need to be fully present to engage the energy of two or more dancers.

# Establishing and Maintaining a Safe Space and Supportive Environment

While there are numerous ways to cultivate a safe space in the classroom, a few key frameworks seem to apply across the board. By giving students agency over their own bodies, fostering open communication, and encouraging an inclusive, nonjudgmental environment, educators allow all students to feel seen, heard, and valued. Embracing equity, diversity, and inclusion, along with endeavoring to increase the sense of belonging and celebration of individuality, sets students up for success with the best conditions for learning and growth.

## Transparency and Open Dialogue

From the beginning of a quarter or semester, a partnering class series, or even a one-off master class or workshop, establishing a culture of open communication and transparent dialogue is vital for cultivation of a safe, inclusive space. When students feel invited to share how they are feeling, to respond to a particular exploration, or to state whether they truly understand a concept, they are likely more willing to try new things. For many dance students, a dedicated practice of dance partnering is often outside of their training experiences and well outside of their comfort zone. Why not hit the ground running by acknowledging this fact openly with the class? Offer it as a broad statement; recognize that the goal is for everyone to feel safe asking questions in class, and state that is always better to ask a question rather than try without a clear understanding of a concept or the mechanics of a skill. Within partnering practice, dancers' responsibility for safety and respect now extends outside of themselves and includes the necessity of just as much awareness of their partner or partners. Another approach is to ask students about their previous experiences with partnering (most students will likely have little prior experience).

Establishing a culture of open communication and transparent dialogue is vital for cultivation of a safe, inclusive space.

As they respond to the question, others will recognize that the students are essentially all in the same place of learning.

In general, I find transparency to be a potent tool in teaching, particularly with the current generation of students. Here, *transparency* refers to open communication with students about the reasons and intentions behind pedagogical decisions. Providing students some insight into the plan and design of one's approach allows them to get on board more quickly or at least recognize that educators often have specific reasons for teaching or introducing material with a particular method of instruction or sequence. Most current students have been educated in the K-12 teach-to-the-test model, which focuses more on the memorization of facts, dates, and calculation steps than on the act of learning and critical thinking. I have seen this manifest in the undergraduate dance classroom as a particular penchant for endgaming and reluctance to participate fully in class discussions for fear of having the wrong answer. When students are programmed to want to know the answer before they even truly know the question, it is often harder for teachers to tap into students' analytical reasoning, critical thinking, and problem-solving. The endgaming I am referring to here comes into play most commonly in the creative series of dance composition courses. I have had students (on multiple occasions) ask me outright what they should include in their composition study (e.g., how many, how long, and so on). Although compositional assignments are framed with prompts and parameters, this mindset eliminates the possibility of spontaneity and recognition of unexpected outcomes that arise from a focus on process.

In the partnering classroom, this dynamic leads to student hesitancy to try new things they do not already feel comfortable doing. At its most extreme, this reluctance can be completely debilitating; even in milder cases, it can lead to superficial exploration of partnering concepts and an inability to let go and trust a partner. Creating a transparent, communication-centered environment can help temper or even eliminate some of this tendency toward reluctance, fear, and anxiety.

Encourage students to work on practicing nonjudgement of themselves and each other. Students will take to some skills and partnering concepts immediately, whereas others may require more time. If students can recognize and celebrate those small victories for themselves and their peers, positive energy and excitement circulate in the space. If the focus is on who did it best, who succeeded, or who failed within a competitive and unsupportive environment, reluctance and apprehension will certainly follow.

One of the most important tools in dance partnering is clear and open communication. This is vital directly with a partner, of course, but it also comes into play when practicing or performing within larger groups. For beginning partnering students, it is crucial that they learn to respectfully but directly ask for what they need and be willing to offer the same responsiveness in return. Of course, this does not mean that a dancer should bully and boss around their partner to make everything more comfortable or suitable for themselves. Rather, they must learn to articulate what connections and types of touch feel clear and confident, or ask for subtle shifts that will foster deeper trust and connectivity.

## Empowering the Individual: Autonomy and Varied Teaching Styles

In his foundational text, *Pedagogy of the Oppressed*, Paulo Freire reflects on the educational practices that many educators were raised with, which often center on a male and Eurocentric model for learning. He explains the shortfalls of the banking concept common to many models of pedagogy: the teacher is the font of knowledge, and the act of teaching and sharing that knowledge is predicated on filling up students as if they were passive receptacles (Freire 2017). Banking is common in formal dance training, with dancers tending to remain silent, absorb the information and material given, and then work toward perfect execution. With this approach, the teacher becomes the most important person in the room. For educators who desire to shift away from hierarchy and imbalanced power dynamics within their classrooms, a change of focus can help achieve that end.

The banking model for education and the master or guru mindset common to dance and similar forms of training (e.g., martial arts, gymnastics, athletics, etc.) are examples of pedagogy with passive reception of information by the student. Freire dives into the theoretical and philosophical underpinnings of this approach to education and deftly compares it to the violence and oppression of colonialism and the negative outcomes of that dynamic. As an alternative, Freire suggests taking a dialogic approach to education, in which the teacher and class cooperatively work toward educating students and gaining knowledge about a subject together (Freire 2017). In this way, students have not only more autonomy and agency but also pride and investment in the act of learning. It becomes an active, analytical, participatory practice.

In contemporary pedagogy terms, the banking model of education described by Freire is now referred to as teacher-centered pedagogy. This approach centers on the educator's knowledge and expertise, and the learning process involves direct sharing of that information. Suggestions for alternative models shift the focus to subject-centered and student-centered pedagogies that move toward increased active student participation in the learning process. Many educators have critiqued and rejected a fully student-centered approach to learning because, in its most extreme form, it may remove lesson plans and course planning entirely. In that model, student whims and interests become the primary focus. I argue that a more tempered and rational view of student-centered pedagogy can be incredibly beneficial for studio-based dance practice, particularly in the study of partnering.

Like many things in life, pedagogy might benefit most from blending and weaving the best aspects of the three models just described. Sometimes, direct absorption of the knowledge a teacher has gained through decades of practice and professional experience is indeed the best way to learn techniques, skills, and mechanics in dance training. Note student interest and curiosity and then tailor the plan of a class or weekly progression to keep students engaged and invested in their learning. This reflexive approach stays true to the learning goals for that progression but allows more time where needed most. Flowing between these models might be the most balanced approach. A quick self-audit can help educators objectively review whether the tactics and techniques used in their classroom are leading to the desired results and serving students in meaningful ways.

By perhaps taking a safe middle ground, I often like to frame my dance partnering and other courses within a subject-centered model. By shifting the focus onto the subject of study and making a cooperative effort to learn about and creatively explore the subject together, a spirit of community, trust, and communication is likely to follow. This approach aligns most to Freire's suggestion of a dialogic model, with the teacher and students coordinated in the pursuit of knowledge. This would simply involve introducing a skill or concept, then shifting toward an improvisatory or exploratory approach for students to practice it. Discussion and peer observation can also empower individual discovery and collective problem-solving when similar challenges arise in a peer's exploration of the exercise. Simply approaching the dance classroom as a laboratory and space for exploration and creative investigation can lead to this more balanced approach and, in turn, foster community and empower students in profound ways.

## The Cowboy Code

Gendered language aside, the *cowboy code* is a light-hearted way to frame a culture of inclusion and belonging in dance partnering practice. I was first introduced to this term and concept when I regularly attended the Big Apple Ranch, a weekly LGBTQ+ country western and line dancing event in New York City. In the period of instruction that preceded the open dance, newer attendees could learn that night's line dance and the basic components of the two-step. During that time, the owner-instructors also encouraged attendees to observe the cowboy code, which was effectively a policy of saying yes and dancing with anyone who asked for a dance. Of course, exceptions could be made for periods of rest, water breaks, or bathroom breaks, but overall, the code encouraged inclusion by rejecting an environment of judgement, selectiveness, or a pick-up culture within the social dance framework of the evening. In that context, the pressure of being asked for a dance as an overture to romantic interest was also removed. Everyone was truly there to dance, to be together in community, and to have fun.

To apply the cowboy code to a dance partnering classroom context, instructors might simply encourage students to partner with different classmates often, perhaps even within a single class. Their default is often to gravitate to peers with whom they feel most comfortable and connected. Although this familiarity may be calming mentally, it limits dancers' physical learning potential. By challenging themselves to connect with and become comfortable with a new partner often, dancers allow the potential for even more information to spring forth. Everybody is different, and every *body* is different. As dancers initially work to understand a concept, certain exercises and skills benefit from learning with someone of a similar size and stature. Yet many exercises and explorations accommodate and even benefit from working with a dancer of a different size, height, or proportion. There is much to be learned relative to degrees of touch and percentage of weight sharing and weight-bearing, access and use of leverage and momentum, and problem-solving benefits of discovering helpful modifications.

## Touch and Consent

Partnering practice can be intrusive and uncomfortable for any student, but it may be even more challenging for individuals who have an aversion to touch. There can be many reasons for this aversion, such as past trauma, heightened sensitivity, oversensitivity, and culturally rooted, religious, or social restrictions on touch. In practice, knowing the reason why is less important (and less intrusive); rather, it is important to be aware of this aversion and the individual's boundaries. Educators cannot read minds, so clearly inviting and giving students permission to express their experience is key to fostering and maintaining the studio as a safe, enriching, and inclusive space.

Open dialogue about consent and safe touch policies within the classroom space can go a long way to ensure that all students feel safe and included. Including touch statements in course syllabi or providing a detailed contract of touch can be helpful if tangible approaches are helpful within the class community. Providing multiple ways for students to communicate the extent of their comfort or discomfort with touch also helps. Some students may feel uncomfortable speaking up inside the group, and they may prefer to speak with the instructor after class or during office hours or even communicate via email. This communication is important at the beginning of a semester or partnering class series, and it is beneficial to include language that encourages active, ongoing reassessment and further dialogue as the course progresses. Some students who are less comfortable with touch initially might open up and become more at ease with it over time; other students who felt comfortable initially may have strong reactions to touch later in the process. Students might be comfortable with peer-to-peer contact but not with contact with their instructor. This is easily remedied and respected by not selecting that student to demonstrate or practice directly and by refraining from tactile correction or guidance, to the extent possible. Creative accommodations can be made when valued in the instructor's pedagogy.

For students with an aversion to touch, narrow their range of partners. Although it is beneficial to encourage students to pair with as many different partners as possible, allowing students with reservations to engage with one or two trusted peers can be a good solution.

I offer the following example to help illustrate accommodation of religious views and restrictions. A Muslim female-identifying student in a nonmajors social dance course clearly communicated to me at the course onset that in observation of her religion, she could not touch or partner with male-identifying classmates. Because the class gender ratio leaned toward female-identifying students, this accommodation was easily managed. Although I could not personally guide the student to clarify or demonstrate material, I coached her and a partner and mirrored her without touch to help in a way that respected her religious considerations.

While these inclusive considerations are important for a safe, consent-based learning environment, it might be unrealistic for a student who has a complete aversion to touch to take a partnering class. Educators must determine their own boundaries and how full accommodation may prevent the student or other students in the class from the learning outcomes unique to a subject.

The sidebar provides sample touch statements that I include in syllabi for my courses. These statements have evolved and expanded over the years, and they have been enriched and informed by meaningful discussions with colleagues and via student feedback and dialogue. These examples are by no means perfect in composition or conception, but they may inspire teachers to craft language that communicates in accordance with their pedagogical practice and social and educational culture.

### Simple Touch Statement for Inclusion in a Dance Technique Syllabus

Touch and physical contact is often used in class—both from the instructor and classmates—as a means of physical input and tactile learning. This interaction is a valuable teaching and learning tool in studio-based physical practice work. If the student has any reservations or aversion to touch or contact, that student should notify the instructor verbally or in writing as soon as possible. Student comfort and the facilitation of their preferred modes of learning is the instructor's primary concern.

### Touch Statement Tailored for the Syllabus in an Advanced Partnering Course

Dance is a physical art form that often requires physical contact with others, particularly for partnered dance forms. At times, the instructor may give corrections for alignment or muscular awareness through gentle, physical contact to help the student understand proper placement and avoid injury. The instructor may also ask for volunteers to work out or demonstrate concepts. Touch is imperative in partnered dancing with other students and is a central requirement of this course. Students may be asked to volunteer to participate in demonstrations of choreographed sequences and improvised explorations (with one another or with the instructor). If you are uncomfortable with physical contact on any level (including by the instructor), please tell the instructor immediately (in person or via email, or some other mode of communication). Consent and physical boundaries are vital to the partnering process, and communication is primary. Please give yourself permission to have an ongoing relationship to consent and boundaries, and realize that these may evolve over time or in relation to particular exercises and principles. These concerns are perfectly acceptable, and an appropriate course of action can then be determined.

## Inclusive Pedagogy

The concept of inclusive pedagogy covers a variety of considerations. In particular, inclusive pedagogy centers on re-evaluating practices of exclusion and emphasizing procedures, course planning, and curriculum design that foster inclusion and equity. Depending on the learning environment, a primary consideration might be intersectional identities specific to race, ethnicity and nationality, gender and sexuality, religion and political affiliation, or health and accessibility.

Although all of these frameworks for inclusion are certainly important to all classroom cultures, gender identity and inclusive language are perhaps the most charged within dance partnering practice. The highly gendered, binary language and training methods of traditional dance approaches are often alienating and exclusionary. Gender-inclusive language that welcomes everyone into the space regardless of their actual (or perceived) identity and expression is vital to cultivating a safe and inclusive classroom environment. Table 5.1 provides examples of gendered language common to dance and education settings and suggests alternate inclusive language. Note that these suggestions are particularly useful when addressing students who have not yet shared names or pronouns. For a class or group of cisgender (not transgender) students who all share that they use binary pronouns, instructors can certainly address them in traditional coded language. Yet even in this situation, the use of balanced gender-neutral language allows instructors to

**TABLE 5.1**    Suggested Gender-Neutral Language for the Dance Studio or Classroom

| Traditional gendered language | Suggested gender-neutral alternatives |
| --- | --- |
| "Good morning, ladies and gentlemen." "Good morning, boys and girls." | "Good morning, students." "Good morning, dancers." "Good morning, everyone." |
| "Do you have any brothers or sisters?" "Do your mom and dad live nearby?" | "Do you have any siblings?" "Do your parents or guardians live nearby?" |
| "Would you like to learn the man's or the woman's role in this duet?" | "Which part or role would you like to learn in this duet?" |
| "Take her hand and support her in a piqué arabesque." | "Take your partner's hand and support them in a piqué arabesque." |
| "Be a man. You should be strong enough to lift her." | "Feel confident in yourself. You have the training to succeed in this with practice." |
| "Man up! You need to dance with more strength and masculinity. Don't be so girly." | "This solo calls for an assertiveness, muscularity, and weighty drive to embody the character. Think about those qualities as you execute the material." |
| "You should feel feminine and womanly. This is a soft, lady-like phrase." | "Approach this phrase with the qualities of delicateness, politeness, and poise. Nothing is performed with too much force or intensity." |

retain their practice and awareness and might also serve as a positive and inclusive model for all students. Although instructors cannot truly change overnight, beginning the work of self-reflection and evaluation goes a long way in meeting goals for improvement with impactful instruction within an equitable and inclusive environment.

## Gender-Neutral Partnering Approaches

There is a common refrain when discussing a lack of partnering training in dance programs, academies, and schools: "We can't teach partnering because we don't have enough boys or men." While this might certainly be a sticking point for formal, pas de deux classes inside traditional conservatory or ballet academy training models designed to directly prepare students for the professional ballet field, a gender-neutral approach to dance partnering is not only possible but also incredibly beneficial. De-emphasizing gender in the beginning dance partnering classroom allows for wider exploration and a broader scope of learning for students. Without the restriction of a particular track or role to learn and the requisite skills, mechanics, and movement attributed to it, students have freedom to thoroughly explore the techniques of lead and follow, supported and supportive, or base and flier within the practice. Students have the autonomy to focus on one of these roles in relation to the skills or exercises in focus that week, or they can shift between positions to learn the technique and mechanics of both sides. This rounded, holistic approach to dance partnering can greatly inform students' full understanding of the required skills and will help strengthen the body accordingly.

When educators predicate the inclusion of dance partnering in their program or studio curriculum, this deprives other students of the opportunity to learn partnering. The skills and outcomes of partnering practice not only prepare all dancers to perform, choreograph, teach, or do other dance-related jobs, but they cultivate confidence, trust, communication, collaboration, problem-solving, adaptability, and awareness. These easily transferable skills would benefit an individual in any number of professional fields or career pathways. The notion that boys or men are necessary for a dedicated partnering practice points to a somewhat one-sided plan for them as well. Speaking from personal experience, I have observed that in many classes, workshops, summer programs, and repertory situations, male-identifying dancers—often in the minority within dance studio and early education programs—are relegated to the role of a forklift on an assembly line. That is, if a partnering class only focuses on the traditional lifts and strength required for one-sided, full weight-bearing, the role of boys and men in those classes often ends with lifting. Even when male-identifying students are part of the community of learners, teachers should consider a more broad and inclusive approach so that all students have the freedom of access to learn all aspects of partnering technique.

## *Learning Both Sides: Supporting and Receiving Support*

Reflexive exploration between supportive and supported roles in dance partnering can be as simple as switching roles within a duet while students are still learning material or exploring a concept through exploration. Early in the investigation of a set of skills, mechanics, and partnering principles, switching sides allows students to learn about their primary role by directly experiencing what their partner is feeling. This two-sided input can then be quickly applied to their experience of the exercise and will rapidly help improve their understanding and execution of the concept or skill.

If switching roles or positions quickly within one class period seems to be too challenging for students, have students first practice a concept and learn a phrase of material during one class. In the next class, students teach their part to a partner, switch roles, and try it out. Continually encourage students to move between giving and receiving support as the term progresses, allowing for more student agency to choose, relative to what is being practiced at that time.

These tactics apply, in particular, when the exercise, skill, or movement phrase uses partnering that is significantly offset from mutual weight or support (as in ballet partnering or ballroom dance versus contact improvisation). If weight-bearing, support, and leadership within duet material is more balanced, set a movement sequence with partner A and partner B roles, then loop and repeat the phrase with dancers switching roles. The pace and timing of such a swap should be entirely based on students' needs and skill sets.

## *Focus on the Character or Role in Ballet Partnering*

In ballet partnering contexts where repertory is involved, the instructor can shift the focus from the gender of the role to the character to neutralize possible discomfort at learning material that is historically gendered. This approach will be most helpful for transgender and nonbinary students to feel included and accepted in the classroom. Using gendered pronouns, even when referring to the role students are learning, can be triggering, upsetting, and traumatic for transgender and nonbinary students. For example, an instructor teaching the pas de deux from *Swan Lake* might frame students' parts as Albrecht and Odile rather than the "man's part" and the "Ballerina" or "woman's part." While teaching and coaching, try to use those character names rather than gendered pronouns (he or she) when referring to a particular part of the duet. This shift in language and messaging takes a lot of practice, but it can be incredibly beneficial if the population has a range of gender identities.

This effort toward more gender-neutral communication can also benefit female-identifying dancers learning traditionally male parts. Even beyond the important consideration of transgender and nonbinary dancers, female-identifying students are often called on to partner up and assume traditionally male roles in repertory or classroom situations. Often, the taller and stronger women in the classroom are tapped to assume a more supportive role in partnerships. Continually hearing an instructor or choreographer refer to the role they are learning or performing as the "guy's part" or "man's role" effectively diminishes them and fails to recognize their effort and contribution to the work. The inverse applies to more petite, lighter-weight male-identifying dancers who are singled out to be lifted or learn a more supported role in repertory. Continually referring to their part as the "woman's role" can be unhelpful and discouraging.

## Identity and Representation

While questions of identity, autonomy, and individuality have been ever present in all aspects of life, the time between the late teenage years and early adulthood seems to reflect a deep and rapid development in the sense of self. Each generation and era has also seen cyclical patterns of both self-definition and a generational collective of shared ideologies and points of view. While this is in no way a suggestion that every generation has homogenous views of self and society, there seem to be broad understandings that relate directly to the time in which individuals come of age.

With Generation Z and Generation Alpha coming of age amid the Me Too, Time's Up, and Black Lives Matter movements, there is a deep commitment to individual autonomy, consent, and social justice. There is a broad commitment to advocacy, activism, and environmental awareness and increasing fluidity in relation to gender and sexual identity. The constant inundation of these intense social, political, and global dynamics also seems to contribute to increasing rates of anxiety and depression among children, teens, and young adults. Similarly, the COVID-19 global pandemic, with its necessary lockdowns, social restrictions, and residual dynamics of isolation, trauma, and fear of touch, has significantly affected physical and mental health. For the generations still forming their identity and increasing self-understanding, the pandemic has had profound effects on the already disproportionate prevalence of anxiety, depression, self-harm, and suicide among youths. Current events related to public health, political polarization, social unrest, and widespread violence and fear all contribute to the growth of these challenges.

Although educators cannot fix the world's problems or even insulate students from such hardships, they can provide a safe and welcoming space, an open forum for discussion about dedicated practice to the art of dance, and meaningful conversation around these and other challenges experienced daily. Teachers can also provide a space that works to uphold the pillars of equity, diversity, and inclusion by continually reviewing and revising their policies, procedures, and pedagogies. With care and intentionality, teachers can foster an inclusive space that celebrates differences and honors students for all that they are and all that they hope to become.

### Self-Representation

The process of getting to know students can be challenging and uncomfortable at times. Educators may find it difficult to find balance being transparent about their own lives and personal identities and interests with those of their students, while maintaining boundaries and mutual respect for privacy. The teacher can begin a course or studio season with a small, nonintrusive assignment the encourages students to share about themselves, while providing room to edit, limit, or extrapolate how much they share.

Minor assignments such as entry self-evaluation surveys or short personal histories or biographies can help. A self-evaluation survey may include short-answer questions related to the content and considerations of a particular course. These surveys can also serve as a safe way for students to communicate specific information about how they identify, their name (if different from that officially logged with the university), and their pronouns. By signaling that students can refrain from answering any of the survey questions, the instructor gives students agency and autonomy to share only what they feel comfortable disclosing. In turn, educators can gain more information about their students than might be obtained with a simple self-introduction exercise. Those verbal exchanges can certainly continue, and they are a great way for the teacher and students to learn names and get to know one another. However, more detailed and targeted information can be gained from brief additional assignments. For example, the sample entry self-evaluation survey in figure 5.1 includes questions geared toward gleaning the skills, mechanics, and experience level of students relative to dance partnering practice. Visit HK*Propel* for an editable version of this form to use, edit, and tailor to a student population or populations.

Essay prompts geared toward informal narratives related to students' personal histories or dance biographies can provide detailed information about their prior experience and training. Responses to these prompts can also offer important insight into how student sees themselves, what they are proud of, and what their goals are, and they provide direction for personal guidance and mentorship relative to students' personal needs where possible. A word-count limit ensures that this first-week writing assignment remains low stakes but also guides students to include the most important information they wish to share.

---

## FIGURE 5.1   Sample Introductory Self-Evaluation Survey

**Course:** Integrated Partnering

**Quarter/Semester:** Autumn 2019

**Class Level:** Junior

**Major(s):** Dance, BA/Earth Sciences, BS

**Name:** Max

**Pronouns:** They/Them

- What previous experience(s) do you have with dance partnering as a practice?
- How would you describe or characterize your relationship to, and interest in, dance partnering?
- What are your personal goals for this course? What are your goals for this coming year?
- Do you have any personal anxieties, fears, boundaries, or limitations when it comes to touch and physical contact? With peers? With the instructor?
- What feedback have you received, or are you aware of in your own practice, about issues in your alignment, posture, strength, and balance?
- Do you have any current or chronic injuries, illnesses, or physical limitations you would like to make me aware of?
- Is there anything else you would like to share?

---

From B. Whited, *Dance Partnering Basics: Practical Skills and Inclusive Pedagogy.* (Champaign, IL: Human Kinetics, 2025).

## Names and Pronouns

Names and pronouns are among the most important self-identifiers. This is more important than ever as individuals increasingly self-identify in fluid and nonbinary terms regarding gender identity, gender expression, and sexual orientation, in particular. Self-identifiers related to race, ethnicity, nationality, religion, socioeconomic status, and political affiliation might also enter the conversation when students feel comfortable and invited to share and to discuss openly within a safe classroom experience. Within dance partnering classes, educators will likely observe that personal and gender identity is top of mind for many students with regard to feeling honored, seen, and respected within the classroom.

Of utmost importance for providing and maintaining a safe and welcoming space is to allow students to tell the name they wish to be called and the pronouns with which they should be referred. Assuming a student's gender pronouns or reading an official attendance list aloud on the first day (when many institutions are still far behind on providing a mechanism for students to update or correct their name and pronouns in official systems) can immediately, even inadvertently, alienate some students. Incorrect pronoun assumption can be offensive, triggering, and traumatic, particularly to transgender and nonbinary students. During high school and college, many individuals are often newly understanding themselves in relation to gender and sexuality. Pronoun mistakes and gender assumptions can be incredibly hurtful for individuals continuing to develop a sense of their self and identity. Allow students with nonbinary or neutral pronouns to feel seen and heard by using introduction surveys or self-introductions with those who are comfortable also disclosing their pronouns. Correct use of pronouns throughout the course, including in direct interactions and even in discussions about students when they are not present, is imperative to fully respecting their identity. Just like learning a new acquaintance's name or other personal facts, remembering and using someone's pronouns accurately takes time and effort.

Some people may use the phrase *preferred pronouns* or *preferred name* when discussing gender and self-identifiers. Although this may seem correct and appropriate, use of the qualifier *preferred* is hurtful or offensive to many transgender and nonbinary people. Stating that something is preferred may suggest that other referents are also acceptable, even if not preferred. Just as the use of *sexual preference* is inaccurate and offensive to many in the LGBTQ+ community, the term *preferred pronouns* can be received in a similarly hurtful way. Avoid this by simply asking, "What is your name?" "What are your pronouns?" For example, if a person introduces themself as Max with *they* or *them* pronouns, that is not a preference but the name and pronouns you should use when referring to them. In the broadest terms, if the teacher's goal is to be respectful, inclusive, and not to cause harm, referring to someone accurately and in line with how they identify is the least they can do. Table 5.2 presents some widely used and less common pronouns that teachers might encounter.

I am often baffled by the people I meet who push back on the use of gender-neutral pronouns when requested to do so. Of course, individuals come from different backgrounds and points of view, but I do not understand why someone's humanity, identity, or self-respect should be a topic of debate. Most people would not hesitate when someone introduces themself: "My name is Susan, but please call me Sue." In our culture, the use of shortened names, nicknames, or derivatives of longer, more formal names is extremely common. Why not extend this courtesy to transgender and nonbinary people in turn? This somewhat simple practice, which requires ongoing improvement for many, is an excellent start toward the many ways teachers might wish to foster and uphold a culture of inclusion, access, respect, and equity within the safe space of the classroom or studio.

TABLE 5.2   List of Common Pronouns, With Conjugation

| Subjective | Objective | Possessive adjective | Possessive pronoun | Reflexive |
|---|---|---|---|---|
| She | Her | Her | Hers | Herself |
| He | Him | His | His | Himself |
| They | Them | Their | Theirs | Themself |
| Ze/zie | Zim/zir | Zir | Zirs | Zirself |

## Incorporation of Guest Artists or Lecturers

Educators can never truly know everything or feel the same level of comfort or confidence when teaching different genres or styles of dance practice, history, or theory. They have their experiences and prior training to draw on and personal and professional knowledge that they can often transfer when teaching a newer area or topic. At the root of it all, they only have a single perspective and cannot speak for the entire field of dance or all those who comprise it.

As discussed earlier in this chapter, inclusion of varied perspectives empowers and grounds students within the classroom learning space. By bringing their varied perspectives and experiences into conversation within the studio, the class can then offer a more diverse range of ideas and points of view. In a partnering class or other survey-style course where several topics are covered, instructors will teach material or skills that are less familiar and more challenging. In these moments, they can rely on humility and transparency with students and explain that it seems important to cover a topic although it is outside their area of expertise and experience. In this way, they can invite students into conversation and community as they explore and consider the new topic together.

If that approach feels like it still falls short of the quality of execution and information the instructor would like to uphold, they can seek peer resources in fellow colleagues, local specialists, or even regional guests that might be able to teach a particular area from a place of clarity and expertise. Doing so also effectively diversifies the content and instruction by including guests with different but complementary perspectives, identities, and experiences. No one can be expected to know everything; for those who presume to, take what they say with some caution. Showing the humility and resourcefulness to reach out to other educators and engage them meaningfully in the classroom will do much to enrich the student experience and continue toward a mission of equity and diversity.

## Diversification of Reference Materials

Another simple but incredibly important step toward diversity, equity, and inclusion in the dance classroom is the intentional diversification of in-class examples, outside readings, viewings, and reference materials. When teachers are new to a topic or practice, they often gravitate toward what is most commonly known, likely choreographers, dances, and information they can speak about most comfortably. Yet when these front-of-mind examples, often within what is considered canon to dance performance, are made up of perspectives solely linked to white, upper-class, Eurocentric artists and artworks, teachers fall short of that diversity, equity, and inclusion mission.

One example of incredible partnering choreography—presented in the ballet idiom, but with an incredible amount of innovation, movement invention, and contemporary aesthetics—is Wayne McGregor's *Chroma* (2006). Originally commissioned by the Royal Ballet in London, the dance has been restaged and reworked with many different repertory companies (McGregor 2006). One prominent restaging was with the Alvin Ailey American Dance Theater in 2013 (McGregor 2013). When I share footage of and interviews about *Chroma*, I often share the Alvin Ailey version or both versions if time permits. By considering two or more versions of the same dance, the instructor can cover a wider range of identities and perspectives, broader representation, and aesthetic comparison between the approach of the dancers and artistic teams of different companies. When multiple versions of a dance exist, teachers should consider what they wish to communicate: (1) the original staging as a standard to which all else is measured or (2) the choreography itself. They should also consider whether there is a more inclusive version that can articulate the dance with just as much impact.

Just as important as the material and content shared directly within a studio-based dance technique course, series, or workshop is the diversity of resources and material curated to frame and supplement the core physical practice. The readings, viewings, music, and other resources that teachers select to complement, ground, and enrich a dance course speak volumes to students in regard to what and who educators value, respect, and acknowledge within the dance field, both current and past. Whether that material is something students can relate to regarding identity or representation can have a great effect on their experience within the class. Educators can never truly be neutral in this regard: to neither acknowledge or counter a lack of diversity and equitable representation in dance education is to endorse and uphold those systems of exclusion and erasure. Taking small steps can have an incredible effect when teachers and dancers look at how far the field has come, while keeping their sights on how much further it still has to go.

## SUMMARY

Although educators cannot control or direct how every student will receive instruction within their classes or how they will (or will not) connect to the material, a mindful approach to managing the classroom space goes a long way toward achieving an overall sense of safety and belonging. Teachers can certainly lead by example, but they can also create opportunities for students to express their own values and desires about how everyone in the room can contribute to the production and maintenance of that safe space. Encouraging and respecting self-identification, modeling inclusion by directing students to meet and connect with everyone in the class as partners, providing clear communication and a rigorous practice of consent related to touch and body contact, and offering selective and inclusive choices for the diversification of reference materials are all constructive considerations toward the production of a safe and inclusive learning environment.

## DISCUSSION QUESTIONS

1. What type of class culture and space do you want to foster and provide for your students?
2. What toxic practices in your own training do you wish to avoid or reframe to create an even better environment for your students?
3. What is your own relationship to touch and physical contact in dance contexts? Has that evolved over time?

See the ancillary materials and resources linked to chapter 5 in HK*Propel.*

# RESOURCES

"The Dos and Don'ts of Cross-Training." 2012. *Dance Spirit Magazine.* Posted February 14, 2012. https://dancespirit.com/the-dos-and-donts-of-cross-training/

Albright, Anne Cooper, and David Gere, editors. 2003. *Taken by Surprise: A Dance Improvisation Reader.* Middletown, CT: Wesleyan University Press.

Bogart, Anne. 2007. *And Then, You Act: Making Art in an Unpredictable World.* London: Routledge.

Buckwalter, Melinda. 2010. *Composing While Dancing: An Improviser's Companion.* Madison: University of Wisconsin Press.

Burrows, Jonathan. 2010. *A Choreographer's Handbook.* New York: Routledge.

De Spain, Kent. 2014. *Landscape of the Now: A Topography of Movement Improvisation.* New York: Oxford University Press.

Franklin, Eric. 2018. *Conditioning for Dance: Training for Whole-Body Coordination and Efficiency,* (2nd edition). Champaign, IL: Human Kinetics.

Kourlas, Gia. 2020. "How an Elite Cross-Trainer is Helping Dancers Stay Fit." *The New York Times.* Posted May 5, 2020. www.nytimes.com/2020/05/05/arts/dance/joel-prouty-cross-trainer-ballet.html

Lavender, Larry. 1996. *Dancers Talking Dance.* Champaign, IL: Human Kinetics.

Marian Bryant, Maya. 2022. "Sustainable Cross-Training for Dancers," DanceNutrition.com by Rachel Fine. Posted April 15, 2022. https://dancenutrition.com/cross-training-routine-for-dancers/

McGregor, Wayne. 2012. "Wayne McGregor: A Choreographer's Creative Process in Real Time." Posted September 2012. TEDGlobal. 15 minutes and 18 seconds. www.ted.com/talks/wayne_mcgregor_a_choreographer_s_creative_process_in_real_time

Morgenroth, Joyce. 2004. *Speaking of Dance: Twelve Contemporary Choreographers on Their Craft.* New York: Routledge.

Olsen, Andrea. 2014. *The Place of Dance: A Somatic Guide to Dancing and Dance Making.* Middletown: Wesleyan University Press.

Paxton, Steve. 1972. *Magnesium.* Grand Union residency at Oberlin College. Video by Steve Christiansen. *Contact Quarterly.* https://contactquarterly.com/contact-editions/title/magnesium-(1972)

Prichard, Robin. 2017. "Redefining the Ideal: Exquisite Imperfection in the Dance Studio." *Journal of Dance Education* 17(2):77-81.

Simmel, Lianne. 2013. *Dance Medicine in Practice: Anatomy, Injury Prevention, Training* (1st edition). New York: Routledge.

# GLOSSARY

**360-degree core**—A fully integrated core comprises the abdominals and lower back muscles (front to back) and the pelvic floor, intercostal muscles, and upper back muscles (up to down) that create a 360-degree initiation and stabilization of the body's core or weight center. By integrating front, back, up, and down, the dancer can support a wide array of movements with safe mechanics.

**ballroom dance**—Formal social dancing performed in couples; improvised in most settings, with lead and follow roles. Codified and choreographed forms of ballroom dance are known as dance sport.

**base of support**—The zone beneath an object or person that connects with a stable surface. This base can be made up of multiple body parts or props and assistive devices like a crutch, walker, or chair (e.g., when standing upright, the bases of support are the feet; when kneeling, these bases are the knees and feet).

**center of balance**—The alignment of the center of gravity over the base of support along the vertical axis; also known as the *plumb line.*

**center of gravity**—The area of the body understood to hold the most density of mass; the weight center of the body. Different bodies hold their weight in different centers of gravity according to anatomical differences. The human center of gravity mostly exists in the pelvis and lower torso but with different anatomical weight distribution in the body, it might include the full torso, lifting the center of gravity higher toward the waistline.

**centripetal force**—The force or action created as a result of rotation around a singular, central point. With even speed or rate of rotation, the weight and force of the person or object being rotated distributes outward along a transverse (horizontal) plane.

**classicism**—Adherence to traditional standards (of simplicity, restraint, and proportion) that are universally and enduringly valid (Merriam-Webster 2023).

**composition**—The second aspect of choreography that includes the development, arrangement, direction, and expansion of phrase material. Like in music composition where melodies and harmonies are arranged with variations and developments of a root theme or base musical phrase, dance composition refers to the arrangement of phrases of movement material beyond their original creation. Formal devices, such as reflection, repetition, retrograde, canon, unison, and theme and variations, are often used in this phase of the choreographic process, following the first phase, *movement generation.*

**consent**—Informed and ongoing permission for an event or action made by an individual with agency and autonomy. Consent is a dynamic of agreement and clearly communicated permission or boundaries between two or more individuals.

**contact improvisation**—An improvised partnering dance form developed primarily by Steve Paxton, along with Nancy Stark Smith, the members of the Grand Union, and other collaborators. The practice is particularly weighted, risky, and acrobatic, with the intensity of weight sharing dissipated by the application of momentum.

**contralateral**—Actions of the body that initiate from limbs or body parts on opposite sides of the vertical midline that splits the body into right and left halves. Walking is an everyday example of a contralateral movement, with the arms and legs swinging in opposition as one walks.

**counterbalance**—The weight of one partner balances the weight of another, characterized by the action of falling away from each other. The partners' bases of support are close to one another, their weight centers fall away, and they are connected by a point (or multiple points) of contact above the base of support.

**court dance**—A stately, noble, aristocratic form of social dance that emerged within the European courts in the 16th, 17th, and 18th centuries. Often drawing from regional, culturally specific, or national dances of rural and suburban Europe, court dance appropriated and formalized these forms for performance suitability in the presence of the monarchy.

**dialogue**—Ongoing, active, and productive communication among dance partners, students, instructors, and peers in a classroom. Dialogue refers to the discussion and problem-solving necessary for effective technique, active and ongoing consent, and safety within dance partnering contexts. Dialogue might also refer to the nonverbal, physical language of duet interaction if one considers dance as a text or a movement language spoken between partners or among a group.

**durational support**—A physical dynamic in partnering characterized by continual, ongoing support of another dancer's weight (in simple terms, carrying one's partner). To achieve uninterrupted and reliable support, momentum and thrust are minimized or avoided entirely.

**eccentric (muscle contraction)**—Engagement of the muscle where the force on the muscle itself exceeds its initiation and elongates the muscle as it contracts (e.g., lowering a heavy object). The engagement of muscles required to lower the object smoothly is an eccentric contraction.

**homolateral**—Actions of the body that originate from the same side relative to the vertical midline that splits the body into right and left halves.

**improvisational score**—In improvisational dance practice, a set of directives or generative plans for the events that will occur within an improvised dance. The directives might signal the steps and order of events, frames, or shifts in time, tempo or duration, location of events on the stage or in the space, qualities of movement and shifts between, or any number of other dynamics. The score is a map or template of an improvised exploration or performance that might be used (1) to generate innovative movement material early in a choreographic process or (2) to create order and logic in a performed improvisation. The rules, parameters, and directives can be extremely specific or broad and open, depending on the intention or the artists involved.

**inclusive pedagogy**—An approach to teaching and education that centers on an ethos of access, equity, and inclusion. Decisions surrounding what is taught and how it is transferred to students center around the effort of inclusion.

**isometric (muscle contraction)**—Describes a muscular action or initiation where the length of the muscle remains the same. The muscle is engaged without movement of the limbs or structures connected to it (e.g., the engagement of extended arms in a plank position, or flexing the leg muscles while they remain long or extended).

**isotonic (muscle contraction)**—Describes a muscular action or initiation that involves a shortening or contraction of the muscles; also known as concentric muscle contraction (e.g., a bicep curl where the contraction of the biceps muscle brings the forearm closer to the upper arm when fully engaged).

**laboratory setting**—An exploratory, process-based frame for the practice of dance. Whether in a classroom setting, rehearsal room, or even a performance itself, emphasizing the work as a site of research and experimentation in dance practice allows for unexpected and surprising outcomes. Although it may seem an obvious frame from dance-making training and creative process, inviting students and professional dancers to remain in a process-based and experimental mindset allows for greater discovery.

**mobility challenges**—Extra movements that challenge the stability of the core (e.g., pumping the arms in a Pilates hundred or touching the toes down while holding an active crunch).

**modernism**—A self-conscious break with the past and a search for new forms of expression. In dance, *modernism* refers to the period that emerged at the beginning of the 20th century and evolved within multiple areas of dance practice (Merriam-Webster 2023). Although most directly related to the emergence of modern dance, some modernist choreographers began pushing the boundaries and questioning the constraints of classical ballet even sooner.

**movement generation**—The initial creation stage of dance movement material. Usually producing sequences of movement referred to as *phrases*, for many, this is the first step in the process of choreography. Movement generation refers to the production of the raw materials, and movement passages that, through the next step of composition, are developed, expanded, refined, and organized.

**neoclassicism**—A period of reinvention and expansion beyond the codified, formal rules of classical ballet. This style included greater use of the torso, expanded the port de bras, and included movement styles and techniques from other forms. This period is often attributed to George Balanchine and his contemporaries.

**plumb line**—The vertical axis through the body that establishes ease of balance. With the body's center of gravity aligned above the base of support, gravity acting on the body is minimized and balance is achieved. Although the simplest form of the plumb line exists in upright postures, an off-kilter alignment of the body can still find balance along the plumb line.

**pluralistic mindset**—An inclusive, collaborative approach in the choreographic process or classroom culture in training. By focusing on the development of the work, or study of the subject, removed from ego-based, singular points of view, this approach allows for the breakdown of hierarchies and fosters a spirit of community and mutual respect of the contributions of all collaborators.

**point of contact**—Parts or surfaces of the body that connect with one's partner. The point of contact might connect to push away and self-support or to grasp and clasp and hang from a supportive partner.

**postmodernism**—A late 20th-century style and concept in the arts, architecture, and criticism that represents a departure from modernism and has at its heart a general distrust of grand theories and ideologies as well as a problematic relationship with any notion of art (Stevenson and Lindberg 2015). The postmodern movement in dance is often credited with the emergence of the American 1960s downtown dance scene surrounding the Judson Dance Group. Similar aesthetic, theoretical, and philosophical shifts in the practice, creation, and presentation of dance were emerging in Europe and in California at the same time.

**practice**—Repeatedly honing a set of skills or techniques. Practice is the laboratory-style, studio-based training inherent to dance education. Practice-based research refers to the act of dance training, performance, and dance making with an embodied intellectual, theoretical lens.

**pranayama**—A dedicated study within yoga that trains, aligns, and expands the use, accessibility, and depth of breath support. Pranayama functions to cleanse the cardiovascular system, center the mind and nervous system, and allow for full, oxygen-rich breath support for asana practice.

**process**—The steps of movement generation and composition that constitute the development of dance choreography. A process-centered approach to choreography refers to dance making that centers more on the process of development over an emphasis on the product or outcome.

**risk-taking**—Often considered as a negative trait, risk-taking in a dance partnering and creative process context serves as a means of exploring the edge of the unexpected and pushes the creative and technical boundaries of dance making and performance. Within a partnership of skilled, technically sound dancers, partnered material with risk exemplifies excitement and awe-inspiring movement.

**social dance**—Refers to the common, communal forms of dancing that occur within cultures, most often in public events, spaces, and gatherings. Some forms have a reflexive relationship with more formalized ballroom dances, and others have emerged from the socially constructed rhythms, perspectives, and cultures of the people. Although social dances are often witnessed by others, their primary aim is for inclusion and participation rather than simple presentation.

**somatics**—The study and awareness of the body (soma-) and its actions, focusing on internal sensation and the mind–body connection. Somatics is a field of dance, physical training, and practice that originates in the body, anatomy, and physiology and is less concerned with aesthetically driven movement.

**student-centered pedagogy**—A teaching style that puts the interests, desires, and needs of the students at the core of its effort; a collaborative, individualistic approach to education.

**subject-centered pedagogy**—A teaching style that places primary focus on the subject, material, or information being taught.

**synergy**—The coordination of linked muscles or muscle groups working together. Synergy is a balanced engagement of a muscle group and its antagonists, muscles that perform an opposing action (e.g., the quadriceps muscles of the thigh that extend the knee joint versus the hamstrings that flex the knee joint).

**teacher-centered pedagogy**—A teaching style that draws the content and information being shared from the knowledge, expertise, and experience of the instructor. This is a top-down model for education that frames the teacher as the giver of information and the student as the receiver.

**touch statement**—A statement of intention, policy, or procedures related to the dynamics of touch and a system for the communication of consent and approval or restrictions and boundaries. The statement might be communicated verbally, reinforced as a shared and accepted culture, posted visually in a common space or classroom, or included in the text of a syllabus or contract.

**traction**—Sustained and even pulling action on a muscle, limb, or zone of the body. A common use in medical practice is traction of the neck or spine to allow an injury, compression, or subluxation to release and heal. When traction is applied to the limbs, the impact and compression of the joints along the limbs are reduced or counteracted.

**weight sharing**—The process of falling off a central axis or plumb line toward one's partner or an upright, stable surface. Weight sharing is the direct opposite of counterbalance in dance partnering; the partners' bases of support are farther apart, with weight centers falling toward one another and with points of connection or a surface of the body providing support. A simple image to characterize the shape of a weight share is a teepee or a tripod, in which the connection to the ground is wide and the connection between structures is at the highest point.

# BIBLIOGRAPHY

Bales, Melanie, and Rebecca Nettl-Fiol, editors. 2008. *The Body Eclectic: Evolving Practices in Dance Training*. Urbana: University of Illinois Press.

Banes, Sally. 1987. *Terpsichore in Sneakers: Post-Modern Dance*. Middletown, CT: Wesleyan University Press.

Banes, Sally. 1998. *Dancing Women: Female Bodies on Stage*. London: Routledge.

Beaumont, Cyril W. 2003. *The Dancing Master: Pierre Rameau*. Translated by Cyril W. Beaumont, 1931. Hampshire, UK: Alton Dance Books.

Burt, Ramsay. 2007. *The Male Dancer: Bodies, Spectacle, Sexualities* (2nd edition). London: Routledge, Taylor & Francis Group.

Chism, Nancy Van Note. 2002. "Valuing Student Differences." In *Teaching Tips: Strategies, Research, and Theory for College and University Teachers* (11th edition). Edited by Wilbert J. McKeachie, 128-147. Boston: Houghton Mifflin Company.

Christensen, Anne Middelboe. 2007. "Deadly Sylphs and Decent Mermaids: The Women in the Danish Romantic World of August Bournonville." In *The Cambridge Companion to Ballet*, edited by Marion Kant, 9-18. Cambridge, UK: Cambridge University Press.

Desikachar, T.K.V. 1995. *The Heart of Yoga: Developing a Personal Practice*. Rochester, VT: Inner Traditions International.

Erkert, Jan. 2003. *Harnessing the Wind: The Art of Teaching Modern Dance*. Champaign, IL: Human Kinetics.

Fitt, Sally Sevey. 1996. *Dance Kinesiology* (2nd edition). New York: Schirmer/Thomas Learning.

Franks, A.H. 1963. *Social Dance: A Short History*. London: Routledge.

Freire, Paulo. 2007. *Pedagogy of the Oppressed*. London: Penguin Classics/Penguin Random House.

Horst, Louis. 1953. *Pre-Classic Dance Forms*. New York: Kamin Dance Publishers.

Kwan, SanSan. 2017. "When is Contemporary Dance?" In *Dance Research Journal* 49, no. 3 (12, 2017), 38-52. Cambridge, UK: Cambridge University Press.

Manculich, Joshua, and Brandon Whited. 2018. "Practical Skills and Inclusive Pedagogy for Dance Partnering: In Practice." Presentation at the National Dance Education Organization National Conference, San Diego, CA, October 5-7, 2018.

McGregor, Wayne. 2006. *Chroma*. The Royal Ballet. Premiered November 17, 2006, Royal Opera House: London.

McGregor, Wayne. 2012. "Wayne McGregor: A Choreographer's Creative Process in Real Time." Posted September 2012. TEDGlobal. 15 minutes and 18 seconds. www.ted.com/talks/wayne_mcgregor_a_choreographer_s_creative_process_in_real_time

McGregor, Wayne. 2013. *Chroma*. Alvin Ailey American Dance Theater. Restaging by Antoine Vereecken. Company premiere, December 2013, New York City Center: New York, NY.

Merriam-Webster. 2023. *Webster's Dictionary*. www.merriam-webster.comwww.merriam-webster.com.

Nevile, Jennifer. 2007. "The Early Dance Manuals and the Structure of Ballet." In *The Cambridge Companion to Ballet*, edited by Marion Kant, 9-18. Cambridge, UK: Cambridge University Press.

Novack, Cynthia. 1990. *Sharing the Dance: Contact Improvisation and American Culture*. Madison: University of Wisconsin Press.

Prichard, Robin. 2017. "Redefining the Ideal: Exquisite Imperfection in the Dance Studio." *Journal of Dance Education* 17(2):77-81.

Serebrennikov, Nikolai. 2000. *Pas de Deux: A Textbook on Partnering* (2nd edition). Gainesville: University Press of Florida.

Stevenson, Angus, and Christine A. Lindberg, editors. 2015. *New Oxford American Dictionary* (3rd edition). Oxford, UK: Oxford University Press.

Wei, Shen. 2004. *Connect Transfer*. Premiered at the American Dance Festival. Durham, NC. 30 minutes. www.shenweidancearts.org/connect-transfer

Wei, Shen. 2007. *Re-Part II*. Premiered at Lincoln Center Festival as part of the triptych, *Re-(I, II, III)*. New York, NY. 30 minutes. www.shenweidancearts.org/re-2

# INDEX

*Note:* The italicized *f* and *t* following page numbers refer to figures and tables, respectively.

# ABOUT THE AUTHOR

© Fritz Olenberger

**Brandon Whited**, **MFA,** is an associate professor of dance in the department of theater and dance at the University of California, Santa Barbara (UCSB). He is the artistic director of Santa Barbara Dance Theater, a resident professional company at UCSB. Earning a BFA from University of North Carolina School of the Arts and an MFA from The Ohio State University, Brandon has studied multiple genres, from social dance and classical ballet partnering to contact improvisation and contemporary dance partnering.

Professor Whited has presented his choreography throughout the United States (New York, North Carolina, Maryland, Ohio, Texas, and California) and internationally (Parma and Castiglione della Stiviere, Italy). He has danced professionally as a core member of Shen Wei Dance Arts (2009 to 2014) as well as with Steeledance, Randy James Dance Works, and Daniel Gwirtzman Dance Company, and he has been a specialized supernumerary with the Metropolitan Opera. Mr. Whited has also worked in musical theater as a performer and choreographer.